SHORT SERMONS
FROM THE
NEW TESTAMENT

REV. DR. JACKSON YENN-BATAH

Short Sermons from the New Testament

Copyright © 2022 by Rev. Dr. Jackson Yenn-Batah.

Paperback ISBN: 978-1-63812-303-3
Ebook ISBN: 978-1-63812-302-6

All rights reserved. No part in this book may be produced and transmitted in any form or by any means, electronic, or mechanical, including photocopying, recording, or by any information storage and retrieval system, without permission in writing from the copyright owner.

The views expressed in this work are solely those of the author and do not necessarily reflect the views of the publisher hereby disclaims any responsibility for them.

Published by Pen Culture Solutions   08/31/2022

Pen Culture Solutions
1-888-727-7204 (USA)
1-800-950-458 (Australia)
support@penculturesolutions.com

Contents

Dedication ix
Preface xi

Chapter 1   Topic: "Who Is Jesus To You?" 1
Chapter 2   Topic: "Faith That Won't Give Up" 7
Chapter 3   Topic: "Focus Your Faith On Jesus. Truly You
            Are Son The God." 12
Chapter 4   Topic: "The Miracle Of God's Provision" 18
Chapter 5   Topic: "Are You A Citizen Of The Kingdom Of God?" ... 25
Chapter 6   Topic: "Are Your Wheat (Saved) Or Tares (Unsaved)?" 33
Chapter 7   Topic: "Which Soil Are You?" 41
Chapter 8   Topic: "Called To Confront An Evil World." 48
Chapter 9   Topic: "Finding Rest In Jesus" 57
Chapter 10 Topic: "The Great Commission "The Way Of Faith" 64
Chapter 11 Topic: "We Need The Holy Spirit" 73
Chapter 12 Topic: "Knowing The Good Shepherd" 80
Chapter 13 Topic: "Overcoming Doubts In Our Lives" 88
Chapter 14 Topic: "Hosanna" Or "Crucify Him" Which
            Side Are You? 95
Chapter 15 Topic: "When Your Faith Is Tested" 102
Chapter 16 Topic: "Judgement Day" 109
Chapter 17 Topic: "Whatever You Do, Do Not Fall Asleep" 114
Chapter 18 Topic: "The Good News Of Jesus Christ" 119
Chapter 19 Topic: "Nothing Is Impossible To God" 124
Chapter 20 Topic: "The Waiting Is Over" 130
Chapter 21 Topic: "Walk In The Light" 136
Chapter 22 Topic: "Have You Been Baptized?" 142

Chapter 23	Topic: "Come And See"	147
Chapter 24	Topic: "Follow Me"	153
Chapter 25	Topic: "Are You Searching For Jesus?"	159
Chapter 26	Topic: "Listen To Him"	165
Chapter 27	Topic: "Life In The Wilderness"	171
Chapter 28	Topic: "What Is True Worship?"	176
Chapter 29	Topic: "The Good News Of The Pole"	182
Chapter 30	Topic: "We Want To See Jesus"	188
Chapter 31	Topic: "The Triumphant Entry"	193
Chapter 32	Topic: "He Is Risen"	199
Chapter 33	Title: "Hope In The Time Of Fear"	204

About the Author 209

──── Dedication ────

This book is dedicated to my son the Rev. Samuel Jackson Yenn-Batah, Manager of Pastoral Care at Penn Medicine Princeton Health, Princeton, New Jersey and the Rev. LaThelma A Yenn-Batah, Senior Pastor of Flemington Baptist Church, New Jersey for your commitment and love for serving the Lord in ministry.
Much thanks and appreciation for bringing hope and inspiration to the lives of many people every day.

Grace and peace be with you always.

—JYB.

Preface

This book titled "Short Sermons from the New Testament" contains short sermons preached during the Covid-19 pandemic when Churches were closed down in 2020 to stop the spread of the pandemic.
The Sermons follow the lectionary readings for the years 2019/2020.

They are short because they were preached online for members of Wesley United Methodist Church in Arlington Texas.

The purpose for preaching these sermons were twofold: to serve as a means for deeper understanding of Biblical faith through sound Biblical exegeses and to challenge listeners to grow into Christian maturity.

I am very grateful to members of my church who inspired me to write and preach these Sermons. My special thanks go to the Women Fellowship President Mrs. Araba Plange, the Lay Leader Mr. Fred Nfodjo and Church Council Chair Mrs. Angela Azu for their support, encouragement and excellent leadership in the Church.

Glory be to the Father, Son and the Holy Spirit.

—JYB.

Chapter 1

TEXT: MATTHEW 16: 13-20

TOPIC: "WHO IS JESUS TO YOU?"

INTRODUCTION: In our text for meditation today, we continue with our reflection on the Gospel of Matthew which is the Gospel reading during this lectionary period for the season of Pentecost. Matthew 16: 13-20 is among the theologically dense text in the New Testament. In short order, it addresses a wide range of foundational truths about who God is, how He works, and who we are as His people. It deals with salvation, the effects of sin on us and on Jesus Christ, and the life of discipleship. It raises issues related to the Church, Christ, Salvation and the Holy Spirit.

In the text, our faith is challenged. We are confronted with the reality of our confession as Christians. The pericope of the text gives us a preview. Jesus led the disciples to the mountains of Caesarea Phillipi and the pagan temple of pan where the "gates of Hades" spewed steam from the rocky cliffs. From this strategic location, Jesus declares the foundation of His Church and describes its formation as a battle, with the gates of Hades opposing the gospel's advance. He points out that every person must declare an allegiance to Christ or the gates of Hades, challenging us whether we will remain loyal to the "Son of the Living God" or be seduced by the pleasures of the world?

And so we see that at a critical point in His public ministry, the Lord Jesus led his disciples on an unusual departure to the northern region of Caesarea Phillippi. Prior to Chapter 16, Jesus spent much of his time <u>addressing crowds</u>, working <u>miracles</u> and <u>verbally jousting</u> with the Scribes and Pharisees. But from Chapter 16 onwards, he spends time instructing the disciples - preparing them for Jerusalem and his cross.

In Caesarea Phillipi, Jesus chooses this gentile place to reveal himself more completely to his disciples. But rather than telling the disciples his identity, Jesus asks his disciples who people believe the Son of Man to be. "Son of Man" is the title Jesus most often used to identify himself.

The disciples, not just Peter, tell Jesus that people think of him as John the Baptist who was murdered by Herod. John the Baptist was such a powerful presence that the people would not be surprised to see him again. Indeed, Herod thought that Jesus might be the resurrected John

(Matthew 14:2)

They say that people think he is the Prophet Elijah, the worker of miracles, who was expected to reappear "before the great and terrible day of Yahweh comes" and some thought he is the Prophet Jeremiah, who had opposed the religious leaders in Jerusalem and had predicted the destruction of Jerusalem and the temple.

It is clear that people thought well of Jesus and pegged Him as a prophet. However, when they tried to identify Him, they do so in terms of past prophets. But Jesus is more than a prophet. <u>He is the Christ, the Anointed One of God</u>.

And now, the question that we must all answer today is when Jesus says: <u>"But who do you say that I am?"</u> This question was addressed to His disciples at large and not to Peter only. The people are free to believe whatever they want about Jesus, but Jesus has been carefully preparing those disciples to carry on his work. They have heard his teachings and witnessed his miracles. What they think of him is critical and so do we.

How we answer the question is very critical. Uncertainty equates to unbelief at this point. If you are not sure of who Jesus is in your life. The truth is that to be a Christian means believing that Jesus is the Christ, the Son of the Living God. Anything else is less than Christian.

Simon Peter answered "You Are the Christ". Christ means "the anointed one". Israel anointed people with oil to set them apart for special role such as <u>prophet</u>, <u>priest</u> or <u>king</u>.

But when Peter said "You are the Christ," he was going one step further. Israel for many years had been looking for God to send a Messiah, a savior like David of old, to make Israel Great Again. When Peter said "You are the Christ", he was saying "You are the Savior for whom we have waited for centuries. You are the one sent from God to save us." A statement like Peter's demands commitment. If he truly believes that Jesus is the Messiah, he will have to give his all to Jesus' service. That is also true for us.

So the question we must all answer today is "But who do you say that I am?" Some of the answers I have heard or read about are: He is my personal Lord and Savior. The Son of God incarnate. He is my life, the song I sing, my everything. My buddy, brother, friend, rock, comforter, etc.

Let me stress that I do not want to answer the question for you. I cannot. This morning, each of us must answer it for ourselves. It is not, however a theological or bible exam. If anything, it is an examination of our own lives.

Jesus is not asking us this question just for us to parrot back the answers we have heard or read. Maybe that is why he pushes the disciples to move from what they are hearing around them - John the Baptist, Elijah, Jeremiah, or one of the prophets - to what they are hearing within themselves. "But who do you say I am?" he asked. It is not an easy question as we may think. Sometimes we settle for what I call "Sunday Jesus" answers: <u>the easy</u>, <u>feel good</u>, or <u>sentimental answers</u>. The problem is life is not always easy, feel good or sentimental. It is one thing to say who Jesus is when we are in relative safety. And it is a very different thing to say when we are outside of that safety.

The question is never merely <u>academic</u> or <u>abstract</u>. It is always has a context.

- Who do we say Jesus is when a loved one dies, when the doctor gives news we did not want to hear, or when our life seems to be falling apart?
- Who do we say Jesus is when Covid-19 is spreading and people are dying, people in our country go to bed hungry, live amidst domestic violence, or have lost their jobs and cannot support their family?
- Who do we say Jesus is when we are faced with decisions that have no easy answers, when the night is dark and the storms of life, overwhelm us, when faithfulness means risking it all and taking stand against a louder and seemingly more powerful majority? Who do we say Jesus is when we are persecuted for Christ sake?

Here is the point. Who we say Jesus is has everything to do with who and how we are and will be? In some ways our answers say as much or more about us than Jesus. It reveals how we live and what we stand for. It guides <u>our decisions</u>, and determines the <u>actions we take</u> and <u>the words we speak</u>. It describes <u>the expectations</u> and demands we place on Jesus.

It discloses the depth of our motivation for and commitment to following him, a motivation and commitment that challenges us when Jesus invites us to take up our cross and die with him: "Then he said to them all, "If anyone desires to come after me, let him deny himself, take up his cross daily and follow me". (Luke 9:23)

Jesus' question is not so much about getting the answer right as it is about witnessing and testifying to <u>God's life</u>, <u>love</u> and <u>presence in our lives and the world.</u>

It is less about <u>our intellect</u>, and more about our <u>heart</u>. It is grounded in love more than understanding.

It moves us from simply knowing about Jesus to knowing him. There is a big difference between knowing about Him and knowing Him.

There is nothing safe about the question Jesus poses. How could there be?

There is nothing safe about Jesus or the life to which he calls us.

Jesus' life and presence among us call into question everything <u>about our lives</u>, <u>our world</u>, the <u>status quo</u>, and business as usual.

That is why we ought not answer the question too quickly, too rashly or with too much certainty. It is not a question to be figured out as much as it is a question to be lived.

"But who do you say I am?" Jesus asks.

Jesus right now is waiting for your answer. Your answer will determine whether you truly know him or you just know about Him. Just as the Father in Heaven revealed to Peter that Jesus is the Christ, the Son of the Living God, may He reveal to you too who Jesus truly is. And when he does, may you live your life as a true believer and follower of Jesus Christ. For the Bible says: "Not everyone who says to me Lord, Lord shall enter the Kingdom of Heaven but he who does the will of my Father who is in heaven. (Matthew 7:21)

The hymn writer John Newton 1725-1807 when he found Jesus in his life, he wrote the hymn "How sweet the name of Jesus sounds in a believer's ear!

In the fourth stanza, Newton affirms:

"Jesus, my Shepherd, Brother, Friend,

My Prophet, Priest and King,

Rev. Dr. Jackson Yenn-Batah

My Lord, my Life, my way, my End,

Accept the praise I bring."

What is your confession and faith in Jesus this morning?

Who is Jesus to you in this life?

May the God of hope fill you with all joy and peace in believing so that by the power of the Holy Spirit, you may abound in hope, in the name of the Father, Son and the Holy Spirit.

Amen.

Chapter 2

TEXT: MATTHEW 15: 21-28

TOPIC: "FAITH THAT WON'T GIVE UP"

<u>INTRODUCTION</u>: In Matthew Chapter 15, we read that after Jesus had yet another "run in" or confrontation with the Pharisees who had come from Jerusalem to scrutinize His actions and criticize His failure to follow the ceremonial traditions of the elders, He and His disciples withdrew to the region of Tyre and Sidon, two Mediterranean Villages northwest of the Sea of Galilee.

From a distance, a Canaanite woman saw, recognized and cried out to Jesus, "Lord, Son of David, have mercy on me! My daughter is suffering terribly from demon possession" (Matthew 15:22). Surprisingly, Jesus did not respond to her at all. He was not "ignoring" her. He may, instead, have been testing the tenacity of her faith. So with a faith that would not give up, she kept crying out to Him - to the point that Jesus' disciples begged Him to send her away!

At that time, Jesus finally did respond to her, telling her that His ministry is only to the children (lost sheep) of Israel. But even this response is enough to embolden her to come closer to Him, throw herself at His feet and beg Him "Lord, help me" (Matthew 15:25).

Jesus then said something to her that seems to our ears as even more harsh and "off-putting". He told her that it is not right for Him to give the blessings that belong to the Children of Israel to the dogs that surround them. With a faith that just would not give up, she told Jesus she believed that He had more than enough <u>mercy</u>, <u>grace</u>, <u>love</u>, <u>care</u>, <u>power</u>, <u>help</u> and healing for the Children of Israel, <u>for her</u> and <u>for her</u> <u>ailing daughter</u>. What a great faith!

Jesus saw her faith, commended her, granted her request and completely healed her daughter, from that very hour.

Her faith was a great faith that called him "Lord" or "Master". Her faith caused her to come on behalf of her daughter. Against all odds, even when it appeared that she was being ignored and even turned away, she <u>trusted</u>, <u>believed</u>, and <u>hoped</u> in Jesus. Her <u>tenacious</u> faith kept hanging on to the hope that Jesus would have mercy and help her, and He did.

This morning the question is: Have you ever felt like you were "at the end of your rope, and just barely hanging on? Perhaps it is a situation <u>at work</u>, <u>a situation with our health</u>, or that of a <u>loved one</u>, <u>maybe your family</u>, or one near you <u>is in crisis</u>.

Does it seem, at times, that God is ignoring you, or at least distant and unapproachable?

It is times such as these, against all odds, that God calls us to <u>trust</u>, <u>believe</u>, and <u>hope</u> in Jesus! Our gracious Heavenly Father welcomes all who come to <u>Him by faith</u>. The Bible says "And without faith it is impossible to please him, for whoever would draw near to God must believe that he exists and that he rewards those who seek Him" (Hebrews 11:6)

God <u>knows</u>, <u>loves</u>, <u>hears</u> and <u>provides</u> for us. He knows what is best for us. God shows His mercy, grace and help for ALL PEOPLE through the cross of Jesus - through his life-giving sacrifice for our forgiveness and salvation of the entire world.

As we live out our faith through trials and testing, our faith grows into the "Great Faith which Jesus commends - a great faith that invites us to come to Him, empowers us to seek Him every day in every situation, and enables us to trust Him completely.

Perhaps, like the Canaanite woman, your faith is being tested today. You have a dire situation in your life that you want Jesus to address for you but your faith is weak, you have prayed for <u>years</u>, <u>months</u>, <u>weeks</u>, <u>days</u>, and still no response from God. So do you give up or do you hang in there, <u>trusting</u>, <u>pleading</u>, <u>crying</u>, and <u>asking</u> God for His <u>mercy</u>, <u>grace</u>, <u>compassion and healing power</u> upon your life? If you give up in this battle, you will surely lose your battle with Satan, Sin, Death and the flesh. You need to press on no matter how <u>hard</u>, <u>how frustrating</u>, <u>how painful</u>, <u>how disgraceful</u>, and <u>how oppressive</u> it may be, God is faithful. He will have mercy and answer you in due time.

So <u>the lesson</u> that this text teaches us is that Jesus honors the faith that seeks mercy. The Canaanite woman had no resentment, no anger about her situation; she only knew that Jesus was the Jewish Messiah who came to heal people, and for some reason, He was in her town. She sought mercy from Him and Jesus responded with emotion "O woman". Her faith was rewarded and she became one of the early Gentiles to enter the kingdom of God.

It also teaches us that Jesus will do miracles in our lives if we have greater faith than those who lack faith.

The basic theme of the passage is that Jesus went into Gentile territory and did this miracle for a Gentile woman who had more faith than the Jews who were rejecting and challenging Jesus' claim. The text is about the <u>grace of our Lord</u>, about <u>faith of people who are in need and about the coming advance of the Kingdom to the Gentiles who will be sent into all the world</u>.

And so for our instructions, we who are Gentiles, saved by the grace of God, must also take the message of grace to the world, to whoever is seeking mercy and will believe. If there is resistance and refusal, we may continue to pray for them as Jesus prayed for Jerusalem, but turned to people who want it, whom the Spirit of God has prepared to receive the message of the Gospel of Jesus Christ.

Our take away this morning is this: Faith in Jesus leads to redemption through Jesus. "For there is none other name under heaven given among men, whereby we must be saved" (Acts 4:12).

Many of the Jewish people missed out on the grace of God because they rejected Jesus. Similarly, many Gentiles throughout the Centuries have come to God through faith in Jesus the Messiah.

The challenge, therefore, for us is to continue to demonstrate resilient faith in Jesus and to receive redemption in His name.

For your reflection, have you experienced the redemption of Jesus from your addictions, for your sickness, your hurt and abuse? Have you received redemption for not loving people, for not desiring to spend time in God's Word, for not wanting to pray, for not caring to share the Gospel, for not giving generously, for not controlling your temper, for not being patient and respectful to others, for not loving your neighbor, for not being a good mother or father, for living in fear and for wanting more stuff rather than God?

If you are,

Look to Jesus and be redeemed. May the Lord God Almighty graciously grant you the faith of the Canaanite woman - A faith that would not give up.

- A faith that trusts in the Savior Jesus Christ.
- A faith that would not let go of His promises.
- A faith that will carry you through your problems and challenges in life.

- A faith that will carry you into the arms of the <u>loving</u>, <u>waiting</u>, Savior in the world to come!

Don't give up your faith. Trust and hope in Jesus. He is alive forever and He is the Answer to all our needs.

May He grant you His mercy, grace and peace now and forever more in the name of God the Father, God the Son, and God the Holy Spirit.

Amen.

---- CHAPTER 3 ----

TEXT: MATTHEW 14: 22-33

TOPIC: "FOCUS YOUR FAITH ON JESUS. TRULY YOU ARE SON THE GOD."

INTRODUCTION: I had a friend during my high school days. One summer, we decided to seek a vacation job at a factory that produced shoes. We got employed. I was sent to the shoe trimming section and my friend was sent to the machine operating section where the shoes are made.

A few days into our employment, an accident occurred in the machine room involving my friend. I don't know what happened but the news was that the machine he was operating cut-off one of his fingers. I remember they took him immediately to the hospital for treatment.

Later when he returned home, I visited him and asked what had happened to him. He explained that while he was operating the machine, he was tired and distracted. He said in a split-second, his finger was accidentally caught in the machine and chopped his finger off.

It was an unfortunate situation that happened because he lost his focus on his job. Think about this. What happens if you are dicing vegetables and get distracted? What happens if you are hammering in nails and lose focus on the task? In any of those cases, you are likely to mess up what you are doing at best, and at worst could actually get pretty hurt. Our Bible lesson this morning warns us to keep our focus on Jesus in this confusing and dangerous world.

In the passage read as our text, Jesus had a powerful lesson to teach his disciples that night on the Sea of Galilee. And that lesson applies to us too. And that is: Your faith, like every component of your life, needs focus. Without focus, there is no faith. Faith's most basic definition is trust, but if your trust is scattered all over the place, it does not actually trust in anyone or anything. Jesus urges us and the Holy Spirit helps us to keep our faith focused on Jesus Christ.

So let us pick up right where our gospel last week left-off.

Jesus had just learned of John the Baptist's death and went by himself to pray over the sad event. But his popularity was rising, and the crowds were determined. They found him, and despite his emotional state, Jesus had compassion on the crowd and taught them. But the teaching started to go long and people needed food. Rather than sending the people away to find their own food, Jesus miraculously provided a full meal from five loaves of bread and two fish. He fed 5,000 men that day, including women and children.

After that, Jesus sent his disciples on, while he took care sending the crowd home.

After the crowd was gone, he finally got the alone time to pray that he had originally been looking for. He is able to pour out his heart to his Heavenly Father in prayer for what seems to be a rather lengthy period of time, as the next time we see Jesus and the disciples together again it is the fourth watch of the night, that is just before dawn.

In the meantime, the disciples are following Jesus' direction <u>to go on ahead of him to the other side.</u>

But on the Sea of Galilee, a storm had come up. While the disciples are fighting the wind and the waves, they see something out on the water. Not something but someone. Their initial reaction is that they are seeing a ghost, for what else could stand on top of stormy waters but a spirit?

If they were not scared by the storm, this sight rocked their core. <u>"Take courage, " he says, "It is I".</u>

As the disciples are being knocked around by the storm, as they are shaking with fear at this thing they see out on the water, Jesus brings comfort by focusing their faith. It is Jesus, but it should not surprise them to see Jesus out on the water, because he is God. Jesus in the midst of the storm takes them back to the Old Testament to Moses and the burning bush. There God promised Moses that He was the One that always had been with them, was with them now, and would be with them in the future, because God is not the God of the past tense. He is the God of the present tense, and will always be there to <u>help</u>, <u>protect</u>, <u>support</u>, and <u>forgive</u> his people. Jesus shows himself to be that ever caring and protecting God by doing something no person could ever do - walking on the stormy sea.

3 Lessons to learn.

1. Today, God continues to be the I am for us as well. We may feel like our lives are a stormy sea, and we are being buffeted by the waves as the disciples' boat was. We may well be in great danger or trouble, filled with sadness and apprehension. But Jesus comes to us in the middle of all that torment and says <u>"Take courage; don't be afraid, I am"</u> And no matter what disaster has come our way, our faith can focus on Jesus. No matter what disaster has beset us, he is able to help with his power, through his Word, and his reminders of his love and forgiveness that is ours.

During this fearful period in the life of the disciples, we see Peter taking the opportunity to focus on Jesus and showed his trust in a remarkable way. He reasoned that if Jesus was able to walk on the water himself, surely

Jesus could let him walk on the water too. "Lord, if it is you, tell me to come to you on the water" (Matthew 14:28), Jesus invites him to come.

We see Peter crawling out of the boat and walking on water, firm as ground, towards Jesus. He walked right up to him, focused on Jesus, all is well. He trusts Jesus to make this happen; his faith is focused on Jesus and on him only. After all, here is Peter's God and Savior. Here is the one who can do anything! What does Peter have to be afraid of when Jesus is with him?

But then we are told Peter saw the wind, took his eyes off his Savior, let lose his focus, and looked around him. And what a ridiculous scene he saw! He was standing on the water in the middle of the Sea of Galilee in the middle of a storm. And he questioned himself: What was he doing? Why was he there? He was going to get hurt, or worse die!

These waves were too much; the wind was too strong! What was going to happen to him? He began to sink; began to drown. And what do we learn from this?

    2. We learn that we all can identify with Peter. We do not always trust God.

We do not always trust that his will is being done and that he is working everything that happens for our eternal good.

We think that our own strength can protect us or can work things out for us. And then we do not know what to do when our own strength is shown to be weak and our power proves to be lacking. This morning, we are being reminded that there are storms of this sea of life that you and I cannot deal with. Those waves are crashing in and threatening to drown us; <u>Sickness</u>, <u>a curse on our life</u>, <u>death in the family</u>, <u>attacks by</u> <u>demons</u>, <u>violence</u>, <u>stress</u>, <u>job insecurity</u>, <u>entanglement in the</u> <u>law with possibility of going to jail</u>, <u>marital disagreement</u>, <u>physical and emotional abuse</u>, and so on.

Perhaps at these times, you and I like Peter, lose the focus of our faith. We are more likely to focus on the problem, rather than the solution to the problems who is Jesus Christ our Lord.

3. So the undeniable fact in life is that <u>Jesus will never let us drown.</u>

Notice what Jesus did. He did not let Peter drown and say: "You really should have trusted me. Sorry." Nor did he even let him suffer a little bit in that water before ultimately rescuing him. No, Matthew who was one of the disciples was an eyewitness to all of this, says that Jesus immediately reached out his hand and caught him.

We see a slight reprimand on Jesus' part "Why did you doubt?" but its tone was not one of scolding but encouragement. "Why doubt? Remember I can always take care of you". Jesus said to him.

We too, like Peter, often lose the focus of our faith when we are more focused on the problems than the solution. At times, we are more interested in showing off our faith rather than showing off the one we believe in. Either way, our attention and focus goes away from Jesus and either focuses on ourselves and our individual strengths or weaknesses or on the problems that then seem insurmountable because on our own they are.

But as we sink into our own seas, Jesus grabs us by the hand. As he pulls us up, we are reminded that while we have lost focus, he has not.

And as he yanks us out of the water, we are reminded that there is forgiveness. And the good news is that, all of us have been forgiven for those times we have <u>not trusted him</u>, and we have been forgiven <u>for the times we have been more focused on our problems than his solutions.</u> And thank God for his love. This morning whatever problems you are going through, Jesus is saying "You of little faith". Why do you doubt my love for you? Why do you doubt my ability to protect and help you? Why do you doubt my forgiveness? And we have no answer because there is no reason to doubt Jesus.

He is faithful in his love as the covenant keeping God, I am. Jesus is faithful in his ability to protect. He is the one who has all power to work all things for our good. Jesus is faithful in his forgiveness because he paid for our sins, even our doubts and distractions, so they are no more than a distant memory.

If there are any sins plaguing you, focus on your saviour who destroyed them. If there are problems weighing you down, focus on your Savior Jesus who takes care of all things for you.

If you are worried about the future, focus on Jesus who will be there to help you no matter what storms may arise in your life.

1 Corinthians 16:13 says "Be on guard. Stand firm in the faith. Be courageous. Be strong"

God's love for us abounds, and is never ending. He loved us so much that he gave his only son to die for our sins, and all we have to do is to accept his gift of faith and to focus our trust in Him.

So, in this challenging times of covid-19, political upheaval, economic disaster, social disruption, fear, uncertainty, gloom and doom, the word of God says "trust in the Lord with all thine heart, and lean not unto thine own understanding" (Prov 3:5) and to commit thy way unto the Lord: trust also in him, and he shall bring it to pass" (Psalm 37:5). May the Lord help us to keep our focus upon him today, tomorrow and forever in the name of the Father, Son and the Holy Spirit. Amen.

Chapter 4

TEXT: MATTHEW 14: 13-21

TOPIC: "THE MIRACLE OF GOD'S PROVISION"

The Miraculous Provision of God

Introduction: The gospel story for today is an old favorite story about Jesus and his disciples that was told over and over again. There are some old favorite stories which are told only one time in the gospels such as the story of the Good Samaritan, told only once; the story of the Sheep and the Goats, told only once; These are favorite, great stories but they are told only once in our Gospel.

But the story for today, about five loaves and two fish, is not told merely once, twice, or three times but four times in its variations. It is the only Gospel miracle which is told in its fullness in all four Gospels - Matthew, Mark, Luke and John.

The feeding of the 5,000 is told in all the four gospels because it captures the truth, the essence of all the people involved, the essential truth about Jesus, the essential truth about the disciples and the essential truth about God.

It was springtime in Israel.

The rains of March and April had come and the land was now fresh and green. The brown hills had soaked up the spring rains and the flowers were blooming and the hills were green again. It was Passover time in Israel. Passover was their great religious feast, like Easter is for us. That meant a holiday from school, and a holiday from work. That meant that people were taking trips, packing their donkeys and going on a pilgrimage to Jerusalem. It was a time of religious aliveness, of fasting and feasting and travelling.

It was also popularity time for Jesus. He had healed people of their diseases and his popularity was becoming big. He was like a rock star and thousands would gather to hear him preach. At this time, we see his disciples had just returned after being sent out in groups of two to preach and offer healing and expelling demons across the countryside. But it was tragedy in Israel. According to the Gospel of Matthew, John the Baptist had just been beheaded.

John the Baptist was great moral force, the greatest spiritual force and the greatest prophet the land of Israel had experienced for four hundred years. He was the person that everyone looked for moral and religious inspiration and he was just beheaded by King Herod. Everyone was stunned by this tragedy, by this enormous loss, including Jesus, who had been baptized by John and is Jesus' cousin.

And so it was grieving time in Israel, mourning time. People were stunned, and Jesus wanted to get away by himself to grieve, to pray, to remember. He wanted to get away to a lonely place and so he got into a boat to sail across Lake Galilee to a remote point, some four miles away, in order to get away from the massive crowds who were following him, to be alone and grieve the loss of John the Baptist.

But the crowd could see from the shore where he was sailing to.

And so the crowds followed along the shoreline, keeping an eye on his boat, and so when Jesus' boat landed, many of the crowd had already arrived. And what was Jesus' reaction to the thousands who had shown up? He looked on the massive crowd with compassion, like they were sheep without a shepherd, like people who were in need of spiritual feeding for their spiritual hungers inside. And so he taught them and healed them.

The day quickly passed. It got to be later long into the day, and one of the disciples said, "Lord, the hour is late and the people do not have any food and we are long way from any villages. Maybe you should send them home now. And Jesus said to Phillip, "they do not need to go away. You give them something to eat" (Matthew 14:16). The Bible says Jesus said this to test Phillip.

Phillip replied: "It would take time more than two hundred denari, more than two hundred days of wages, and even that would not be enough bread to feed all these people." Jesus said, "Look around the crowd and see what you can find."

Andrew found a young boy with five loaves of bread and two fish and brought the boy, the fish and bread to Jesus.

Jesus invited them to be seated on the green grass. He had them sit in groups of 100 or 50. Jesus took the bread - looked to heaven - gave thanks - broke it - gave it to his disciples - who gave it to the crowds. And they all ate and were all satisfied and there were twelve baskets left over. The number who ate was five thousand men, plus women and children.

This story about the feeding of the five thousand with five loaves of bread and two fish, captures the essence of why it is told over and over again.

The story captures the very essence of Jesus as the wondrous Son of God.

It captures the essence of God's abundant and extravagant generosity and grace.

And it captures the essence of his disciples who had no faith in their Lord as a source of supply, even after they had seen first hand, God's miraculous work in their lives. For us Christians, as we read the story of the feeding of 5,000 people with five loaves of bread and two fish, we can learn four things that can encourage us when the problems we are facing in life seem too big for us.

1. <u>First, we learn we can always count on the compassion of Jesus Christ to address our problems</u>. Notice that Jesus performed this miracle on the heels of facing great grief. He had just lost his beloved cousin and friend John the Baptist who had been killed at the order of Herod. Yet Matthew 14:14 says he had compassion on the people who had followed him. He had such great love, even in the midst of facing his own loss. He knew his time on earth was short. He pressed forward to do all that God called him to do, even when it seemed difficult. And he is still the same today. He knows the pain and struggles we face. He understands. He is never too busy, or too distant to care. He knows the grief we feel each day, for he felt it too. His word says "He is near to the broken hearted, and saves those who are crushed in spirit" (Psalm 34:18). If you are grieving because of a loved one, Jesus grieves with you.

2. Second, we learn that Jesus is bigger than any problem we face.

When his disciples came to him with the problem, he instructed them to "give them something to eat". (Verse 16). In other words, he encouraged them to look for a solution, to take their eyes off the pressing problem and put them on the answer. Jesus is still the Answer to every problem we face today. In a world filled with darkness and fear, he is the only solution for the troubles that surround us.

And he sends us out, in His power and His Spirit every day to live our lives as the salt and the light of the world. To give people something, the very bread of life (Jesus) who can make eternal difference in their souls. This truth remains: "Greater is He who is in you, than he who is in the world". (1 John 4:4). If you cast all your problems upon him, He is bigger than your problems. He will take away your burdens.

3. Third, we learn that Jesus asks us to bring Him all we have.

He asked the disciples to give Him what they had (Verse 18). The little boy whose very smart mom had packed his lunch that day, gave all he had 5 loaves and 2 fish. He offered it all up, though it seemed so meager.

The disciples might have thought Jesus was crazy to even ask for it. Among 5,000 plus people, this would hardly feed even one family. But they still obeyed act ushered the way for Jesus to perform that amazing miracle story still talked about today.

The truth is that: obedience paves the way for great things to happen. Jesus desires our hearts to be fully yielded to Him, and great miracles can occur as a result. Matthew 22:37, encourages us to "Love the Lord your God with all your heart and with all your soul and with all your mind".

Today, if you bring your problems, job situation, unemployment, sickness, poverty, worries, broken heartedness, marital conflicts, fears and troubles to Jesus, he will solve them for you. He is the Answer.

4. Fourth, we learn that Jesus can bring blessings and life from what is broken.

Jesus, our Lord and Savior is the worker of miracles. He is a loving provider. He took what they gave to him and offered it before God.

He gave thanks, blessed it, and broke it (Verse 19).

What powerful words; because if we have ever walked through broken times, we know that however hard it is at the time, there is also great blessing and power that can come through it.

Jesus takes our broken lives, broken pieces and all, and brings us before the Father. That is the grace and favor that He alone can bring into our lives in the midst of dark places. Today, as we come for Holy Communion, let us remember that there was another time Jesus gave thanks before the Father and broke bread with his disciples, it was the Last Supper. And it was the very picture of what He was willing to endure on our behalf - the brokenness of the cross, and the blessing and power of the resurrection.

"While they were eating, Jesus took bread, and when he had given thanks, he broke it and gave it to his disciples, saying, "Take and eat, this is my body" (Matthew 16:26).

I pray that no matter where we are today in life right now, He would take what we offer up to Him, all our brokenness and pain, all our loss and short supply, all our inadequacies and doubt, and that He would breathe His blessings and favor over it, multiplying greatly all that we offer in the name of the Father, Son and the Holy Spirit.

So the most important lessons we learn from this miracle of feeding 5,000 people with 5 loaves of bread and 2 fish are:

1. We can always count on Jesus' compassion for us.
2. No problem in our lives is bigger than Jesus if we bring it to Him.
3. Jesus wants us to bring to Him all we have because He is the Answer to all our problems.
4. Jesus can repair our brokenness and make life new for us.

The question is,

- Have you brought your meager broken pieces to Jesus? Your suffering, loss, trouble, grief, temptation, trials, persecution, brokenness, uncertainty, and fear to Jesus?
- Have you brought your 5 loaves and 2 fish to Christ?
- Your tithes and offerings?
- When we bring our meager resources to Jesus Christ, and it passes through the hands of Jesus, it becomes enough - more than enough abundant blessings.
- When we bring our meager little selves to Jesus Christ, it is absolutely miraculous what miracles and wonders God can do through us.

This morning, what is holding you back from surrounding yourself and giving your gifts, your 5 loaves and 2 fish to God? My prayer is that no matter where you are today in life, Jesus will take what you offer to

Him, all your brokenness and pain, all your inadequacies and doubt, all your struggles and fears, and breath His blessings and favor over you, multiplying greatly all that you offer to Him in the name of the Father, Son and the Holy Spirit. God bless you. Amen.

Chapter 5

TEXT: MATTHEW 13:31-33, 44-52

TOPIC: "ARE YOU A CITIZEN OF THE KINGDOM OF GOD?"

INTRO: Greetings in the name of our Lord Jesus Christ. For the past few Sundays, we have been dealing with the parables of Jesus concerning <u>God's plan of Salvation</u>, <u>the work of</u> <u>Satan</u> and the <u>fickle nature of the human heart</u>. Today, we shall look at the parables that deal with the greatness of the Kingdom of Heaven or God.

In our text, the collection of parables deals with the Kingdom of Heaven. These parables do not describe the Kingdom in a systematic way, but show us a series of snapshots taken from different perspectives. No single picture is definitive, but each provides a glimpse that adds to our understanding.

As we can observe, these parables of the Kingdom of Heaven are paired together.

Firstly, the Parable of the Mustard Seed and the Yeast contrast small beginnings with their great effects, emphasizing the power of God's action. <u>They are addressed to the Crowd.</u>

Secondly, the Parables of the Hidden Treasure and the Pearl have to do with objects of great value which spark great commitment. They are addressed to the disciples. And thirdly, the Parables of the Net and the Parable of Wheat and Tares (Chapter 13: Verse 24-30 - last week Gospel reading), emphasize the present openness of the Kingdom to all who would enter and the great judgment to come in which the bad will be separated from the good.

In the parable of the mustard seed, we are told that the Kingdom of Heaven is like grain of mustard seed, which a man took, and sowed in his field; which indeed is smaller than all seeds", but when it is grown, it is greater than the herbs (Matthew 13: 31-32).

This parable offers hope, promising great outcomes from small beginnings. Jesus intended to encourage the first disciples, who faced daunting odds, and this parable continues to encourage disciples today because most of the church's work today gets done in suspicious circumstances. Our mission seems overwhelming, and our resources seem too few. But Jesus promises that God's power makes everything possible.

The parable of the Mustard Seed and the heaven encourage us to exercise faith and patience. God is less likely to sweep through the world like a conquering hero on a handsome stead and more likely to be found in a still small voice. In most cases, we will see only small evidence of progress - a couple married in the Church, a child baptized, a youth group engaged in activities that look more like entertainment than serious discipleship activities. But in God's hands, these small beginnings have potential to grow so large as to shift the world on its axis.

The parable of the yeast encourages us, not to seclusion, but to be involved in the world. Yeast can do its work only when mixed into a large quantity of raw dough. Otherwise, it is useless. So it is with those who would serve

Jesus. He calls us to go into all the world, making disciples, baptizing and teaching (Matthew 28: 19-20).

But we cannot do kingdom work if we are not citizens of the Kingdom of God. So the question is: What is the Kingdom of God?

The terms Kingdom of God and Kingdom of Heaven are frequently found in the Bible and contemporary Christian usage.

The primary meaning of Kingdom (Malkuth) (Hebrew) and (Basileia) (Greek) means the <u>authority</u>, <u>reign</u>, or <u>rule of a</u> <u>king</u>.

The Kingdom of God is the sphere of God's rule, for the Bible says dominion belongs to the Lord and he rules over the nations (Psalm 22:28). Though nations are rightfully under God's rule, fallen human beings nonetheless participate in what is called universal rebellion against God and His authority (1 John 5: 19). However, by faith and obedience, men and women turn from their rebellion, and are regenerated by the Holy Spirit, and become part of the Kingdom of God and its operation.

While participation in the Kingdom of God is not compulsory, the Kingdom is present, whether or not people recognize and accept it.

<u>A careful study of the Old Testament</u>, shows that the "Kingdom of the Lord" occurs once in the Old Testament "malkuth yahweh" (I Chronicles 28:5). Throughout the Old Testament, but especially in the Psalms and the Prophets, the idea of God as King ruling over His creation and over Israel is clearly expressed. Although Kingship is evident in the Old Testament, there is also a strong emphasis on a future fulfilment of God's universal rule. In Daniel 4:34, he describes God's rule as "an eternal dominion and a kingdom that endures from generation to generation".

When we come to the New Testament we see that while the idea of the universal rule of God permeates the Old Testament, the Kingdom of God takes an additional meaning and importance in the teaching and ministry of Jesus that begins with the proclamation, "The Kingdom of God is near" (Mark 1:15, Matthew 3:2, 4:17).

Although Jesus never specifically defined the Kingdom, He illustrated it through parables in Matthew 13 and Mark 4 and demonstrated its presence and power in His ministry through miracles. He instructed His disciples to proclaim the nearness of the Kingdom as He sent them out in missionary ministry (Matthew 10:7, Luke 9: 10:9,11). In the New Testament, every description of Jesus Christ as Lord is a reminder that Christ is the ruler of the Kingdom of God. This Kingdom of God is both a present reality and a promise of future fulfillment. The kingdom of God was present on earth in the person and acts of Jesus during the time of His incarnation (birth).

After the resurrection, the Risen Christ is present by His Spirit, and where His Spirit is, the kingdom is present.

While the kingdom is manifested in the Church, the Kingdom is not limited to the Church. The fulness of the kingdom awaits final apocalyptic arrival at the end of this age (Matthew 14:27, 30-31).

So when the Bible talks about the Kingdom of God, what does it mean?

Well, the meaning of the word "Kingdom" according to the Bible, must have five ideas in play in order to understand the kingdom.

First, we have to believe that there is a King. There is no kingdom without a King. As the pages of the Bible unfolds, this King starts with Yahweh, the God of Israel and eventually Jesus is on the throne and he is the King and the Father is the King. So we have to have a King.

Second, we have to have a rule.

This King rules. This King rules in two ways:

He rules by redeeming people, by rescuing people so that the ultimate act of redemption in the Exodus or the ultimate act of redemption on the cross is part of what the word Kingdom ruling means. So there is a king and a king who rules first by redeeming and then secondly by governing. Therefore, the whole idea of Lordship is that God is King over his people, they submit to His will and do His will, and that is fundamentally what kingdom means. So notice, we have a king who rules. This King is Jesus and He is ruling by saving and by Lording it over his people by being their Lord.

Thirdly, wherever the word kingdom is used in the Bible, it always means a people. And this people in the Old Testament is Israel and the people in the New Testament is the Church. In the Bible, the kingdom people are those who have been redeemed by the King and have forced themselves under the Lordship of that King. So, for there to be a kingdom, there has to be a king ruling over his people.

Fourthly, the king has a will, a law.

In the Old Testament, it is the Torah, the first five books of Moses, Genesis, Exodus, Leviticus, Numbers and Deuteronomy, in the teachings of Jesus which is located in the Sermon on the Mount (Matthew Chapter 5-7), and in the Apostle Paul, we locate in his teachings of Christian ethics towards the end of his letters of life in the Spirit, And the Kingdom is people who are under that King who has redeemed them and is their Lord and who are following his will.

Lastly, the idea of the kingdom in the Bible is that there is a land. If we read the Old Testament, we will realize how important the land promise is to Israel. There is no king who does not have space to rule in. A king in the Bible is Yahweh, it is Jesus who is ruling over his people by saving them from their sins, and calling them to live under him. He reveals his will to them so that they will understand it and practice it. And then he calls them into a sacred space, in the Old Testament the l ana promise as it moves into the New Testament, it becomes a universal promise as the people of God take up territory and space and concrete incarnational existence throughout the world and they then fulfill the land promise throughout the whole earth. So in the Bible the kingdom of God means the kingdom has a king, a rule, a people, a law and a land. The king is Jesus, He rules over his people, they live under his law and take up space both on earth in

Heaven. Now that we understand the Biblical meaning of Kingdom, let us look at the state of the Kingdom now in our lives.

When the Pharisees asked Jesus at what time the Kingdom of God would come, He answered: "The Kingdom of God is within you, in the midst, or among you (Luke 17:21). At this time, Jesus was intimating that the restored reign of God was soon to be reality, for the One who was to reclaim the usurped territory of God was on earth to accomplish His work of redemption. The overthrow of Satan's dominion had already begun.

Today, the redemption work is complete, yet the reality of the ultimate kingdom is qualified. In the present age, the power of the Kingdom does not halt aging or death. Though God at times miraculously overrules natural laws by sovereign act or in response to the prayer and faith of believers, the Kingdom still works through fallible human beings.

The Church has a powerful healing influence on the world, but final restoration will not come prior to the Second Coming of Jesus Christ. Righteous political and social actions vitally enhance public life, but the main thrush of <u>the Kingdom is</u> <u>the spiritual transformation of persons who together form</u> <u>the body Christ</u>.

The millennium and the ultimate expression of the Kingdom will not come without the physical return of Jesus Christ to the earth (Luke 21:31). So the kingdom is already present, but not yet completed. It is both present and future.

In the interim, between the first and the second advents of Christ, the present age is marked by forceful spiritual confrontation between the power of the Kingdom and the power that dominates the world in this present age. Putting on the full armor of God, believers are asked to engage the forces of darkness: "For our struggle is not flesh and blood but, against the authorities, against the powers of this dark world and against spiritual forces of evil in the heavenly realms. Therefore, put on the full armor of God, so that when the day of evil comes, you may be able to stand your ground, and after you have done everything, to stand" (Ephesians 6: 12-13). We must understand that God has not guaranteed total and instant success in this conflict. Each victory over sickness, sin, oppression, or demonic powers is a reminder of the present power of the Kingdom and of the final victory to come, a victory made sure by the resurrection of Christ. We are called to wage war against sickness, but face the reality that not everyone we pray for gets well. We are encouraged not to surrender to the evil and struggles of the present order; and neither should we rage against God or blame others when every request is not granted. The essence of the Spirit-filled life is to move against the forces of darkness, fully aware that total deliverance is always possible but does not always come immediately. (Romans 8: 18-23). Some of the heroes of faith in (Act 12:2, 2 Cor. 11: 23, Hebrews 11) suffered even death, having their deliverance deferred to a future time. So we should not give in to the ravage of evil, in this world under any circumstances. As instruments of the Kingdom in the present age, we are to faithfully battle against evil and suffering, and wait for the rapture of the Church, the coming of Christ for His own. When he comes, he will set in motion the events that lead to the consummation of the eternal kingdom. The king dom of the world will become the kingdom of our Lord and of His Christ, and he will reign for ever and ever (Rev 11:15).

The question to us this morning is: Are you a citizen of the Kingdom of God?

If you are not a citizen of the kingdom of God where Jesus is Lord and King and rules over His people you can take steps to gain your citizenship in the Kingdom of God today through the following steps.

1. You must come to Jesus through conviction of sin. David said "For I know my transgressions, and my sin is ever before me" (Psalm 57:3)
2. Come through repentance: The bible says "He who conceals his transgressions will not prosper, but he who confesses and forsakes them will obtain mercy" (Proverbs 28:13)
3. Come confessing your sins. 1 John 1:9 says "If we confess our sins, he is faithful and just, and will forgive our sins and cleanse us from all unrighteousness.

4. <u>Come by accepting Jesus Christ as your personal saviour</u>. Roman 10:9 says "If you confess with your lips that Jesus is Lord and believe in heart that God raised Him from the dead, you will be saved.
5. <u>Come through baptism by water and by the Holy Spirit</u>. In Acts 2:41, we read: So those who received his word were baptized, and they were added that day about three thousand souls"
6. <u>Lastly, come by growing into Christian maturity</u>. "For whatever is born of God, overcomes the world; and this is victory that overcomes the world, our faith" (1 John 5:4).

Always remember that

- The Kingdom of God, has a King - Jesus is the King
- The Kingdom of God has a Ruler - Jesus is Ruler
- The Kingdom of God has a people - People who are saved
- The Kingdom of God has a law - The Word of God
- The Kingdom of God has a land - On Earth & In Heaven.
- To enter or become a citizen of this kingdom, you must be born again.

If you are not sure that you are a citizen of the Kingdom of God, this morning, you can gain your citizenship by accepting Jesus Christ as your personal Savior. <u>Come to Him and He</u> <u>will receive you</u> in the name of the Father, Son and the Holy Spirit. Amen

Chapter 6

TEXT: MATTHEW 13:24-30, 36-43.

TOPIC: "ARE YOUR WHEAT (SAVED) OR TARES (UNSAVED)?"

Introduction: Last Sunday, we touched on the parable of the sower. We explained that a parable is "an earthly story with a heavenly or spiritual meaning". We also said it is a comparison of two subjects for the purpose of the unknown in order to teach something spiritual. We said a parable holds the attention of the hearers, enables them to see themselves and while dealing with something well known, adds a twist which fascinates and makes the hearer reflect.

Today, we focus again on another parable in the same chapter 13 of Matthew. In this chapter, Jesus gives no less than 8 parables. In these "earthly stories" with "heavenly meanings", Jesus speaks about God's plan of <u>salvation</u>, the <u>work of Satan</u>, <u>the fickle nature of the human heart</u>, and <u>the greatness of the</u> <u>Kingdom of Heaven</u>.

After Jesus had finished telling the first four parables, the disciples came to Him to ask Him a question. We notice in Matthew Chapter 13: Verse 36, that they did not ask about the parable of the sower, the soils or the seed; they did not ask about the mustard seed or the leaven. When they asked Jesus to explain a parable, they asked Him to explain the one that is the focus of our attention this morning; the parable of the Wheat and Tares. Why did they choose this one over all the others? Well, the Bible does not tell us but it can be assumed that his parable contained some element or something that troubled the twelve disciples.

II. Context: By way of introduction, let us examine this parable using Christ's own explanation of it and notice some reasons why this parable, of all the eight He told that day, caught the attention of the disciples. The context is that a farmer plants a wheat field. He uses good seed and plants the crop expecting a good harvest. However, while he and his servants slept, his enemy entered his field and planted weeds among the wheat.

What are "tares", you ask? Basically they are weeds that go by the name "Bearded Darnel". In the early stages of its development, it looks exactly like wheat. It is only when the plant has matured and the Kernels have formed in the head of the genuine wheat plant that the two plants can be told one from another. The truth is that the wheat has fruit in its head while the head of tares is filled with little black seeds. So the field looks good, the farmer is getting excited about harvesting a bumper crop. It seems there is more wheat growing than expected. However, as the harvest grew nearer, it became apparent there were tares among the wheat. The servants discover the tares and come in to tell the master about the problem.

You see, they were able to tell the difference because as the wheat develops, the kernels grow inside the head of the wheat plant, the weight of the kernels causes the wheat stalk to bend, making the head appear to be bowing toward the earth.

The tares, on the other hand, have light heads and they continue to stand straight and tall.

The servants see the problem and offer to pull up the tares, but the master, knowing that the roots of the tares have intertwined with those of the wheat, forbids them. He knows that if the tares are pulled up, that much of the wheat will be uprooted along with them. His counsel is to let them grow together until the harvest, then he will send in the reaper to gather the tares first and bind them to be burned. Then the wheat will be gathered and placed in his barns.

In explaining this parable, Jesus gives His disciples, and us, the identities of those involved in the story.

1. The Farmer is Christ
2. The good seed is the Gospel of grace.
3. The one who sowed tares is the devil
4. The wheat are those who are saved.
5. The tares are those unsaved but have the appearance of salvation.

The tares are those in the Church who look saved, act saved, sound saved but who are in truth deceived about their salvation. The tares are those who expect to go to heaven when they die, but will, in fact, go to hell! You see, just like tares, lost sinners, even those who act saved, are good for one thing and one thing only, and that is to be burned.

I am sure I am preaching to someone today who is tare. You think you are saved. You hope you are saved, you know the lingo of the Church, you look saved and act saved as anyone around you, but you have never really been born again. There is hope for you to be saved.

The objective of the lectionary this Pentecost season is to win souls for the Kingdom of God. Hence these parables.

So the objective of preaching this message is to get each of you to do what the Apostle Paul commanded the Corinthians to do in 2 Corinthians 13:5. "Examine yourselves, whether ye be in the faith; prove your own selves. Knows ye not your own selves, how Jesus Christ is in you, except ye be reprobates? And to do what the Apostle Peter told his readers to do in 2 Peter 1:10.

"Wherefore the rather, brethren, give diligence to make your calling and election sure: for if ye do these things, ye shall never fall".

The question may come this morning, Pastor, why are you preaching this message to us?

The answer is I love you. I don't want you to go through life being deceived about your salvation and ending up in hell! I have an obligation to obey the Lord who called me to preach. Listen to what he says to me and to all the preaches:

"When I say to the wicked, You shall surely die; and you give him no warning, nor speak to warn the wicked from his wicked way, to save his life, that same wicked man shall die in his inequity, but his blood I will require at your hand" (Ezekiel 3:18)

Therefore, I want to be sure that you are saved by the grace of God. So the question is: Are you wheat saved or are you tares? Not saved?

I want you to think about this. In America, there are over two hundred million people recorded as Church members. If they are all saved, then why is there crime, abortion, drinking, drugs, sexually immorality, and hellish living in our society with violence, hatred and killings? If they are all saved, then why do people who claim to be saved have premarital sex at the same rate as the world? The truth of the matter is that people often think that they are wheat when they are in fact tares. Please let the Lord speak to your heart today. If you are saved, this message won't hurt you; but if you are lost, it could be the tuning point of your life.

In the parable, we notice that both the wheat and tares share common experience of having been planted. The difference in the experience is revealed in two <u>important ways</u>.

First, it is revealed in the character of the seed.

Obviously, the wheat seed produced wheat while the tare seed produced tares.

On a spiritual level, the "seed" is that thing that we placed our faith in. We place our faith in the Gospel of grace. For the genuine believer, the seed is the Gospel of grace. The truly born again person is trusting Jesus Christ alone for his or her salvation.

The tares on the other hand, may be trusting in any number of <u>emotional</u>, <u>spiritual</u>, or <u>physical experiences for their</u> <u>salvation</u>.

It all comes down to where you have placed your faith. What are you trusting in your salvation? This morning?

Do not trust in the assurances of others when it comes to your eternal destiny. Not even your pastor, friends, relatives, parents should convince you that you are safe. What we need to understand is that salvation only comes to a heart that has been convicted of sin and after a genuine repentance has taken place. John 6:44 tells us it is impossible to be saved until the sinner has been drawn to God. The question that we must all answer today is: Where is your faith? On what do you base your hope of heaven? It must be in the Gospel, that is, in the death and resurrection of Christ's atoning work at Calvary, or your faith is in vain. The hymn writer puts it in a better perspective.

He writes:

> My hope is built on nothing less
> Than Jesus' blood and righteousness
> I dare not trust the sweetest frame
> But wholly lean on Jesus' name.
> On Christ the solid rock I stand
> All other ground is sinking sand.
> All other ground is sinking sand.

Be sure your faith is in the right one.

It is revealed in the Character of the Sower

The good seed was sowed by the owner of the field, the tares were sown by his enemy. <u>Why did the enemy do this?</u> Obviously it was in an effort to turn the crop and ultimately, it was an attack on the farmer.

Satan is in the business of sowing tares among the Lord's wheat. Why? Well, he knows that if he can place enough artificial Christians among the genuine Christians, then he can devastate the entire crop. Satan is in the business of undoing all that the Lord is doing.

If he can fill the church with lost church members, then he can fill hell with a multitude of deceived people. If he can mix enough goats among the sheep, then he can disrupt the harmony and the blessedness of the Church.

Wherever there is Church trouble, you can almost bank on this truth: there is a lost person involved somewhere.

Satan knows that enough lost people in the Church will give the Church hell and a bad name. Why? Because the lost can only imitate the saved for so long, then their true nature, like the tares will come out.

So my message is that you need to be sure beyond any shadow of a doubt that you have truly trusted Jesus Christ and Him alone for your salvation and do not allow Satan to deceive you.

<u>Conclusion</u>: So what are the major lessons in His parable?

Notice that both seeds were planted to settle, both progressed together and both were processed together in verses 26-30.

- Lesson 1: It is interesting that, both the wheat and the tares grow together. As the wheat grows, so the tares grow alongside them. They did everything the wheat did and they looked good doing it. But it is pretty obvious that saved people grow in the Lord. If they stay in church, stay in the bible and stay in prayer, then they are going to grow and prosper in the things of God.

The unfortunate thing is that it is also possible for the lost church member to grow in the things of the Lord and still be lost because it takes the right kind of spirit to understand the deep truths of the Bible. 1 Corinthians 2:14 says "But the natural man receiveth not the things of Spirit of God; for they are foolishness unto him; neither can he know them, because they are spiritually discerned." The lost person can certainly understand the Bible. They can memorize it and know the bible stories. They can possess all the activities of the genuine believer. Tares in the Church sing in the Choir, they serve as leaders of the Church, they are Sunday school teachers, they attend Church faithfully and come to prayer meetings. They even stand in the pulpit and preach the Word of God. But because they have all the activity of the wheat, that does not mean they are real. Watch out, do not be a tare.

- Lesson 2. <u>There was the appearance of wheat</u>.

The parable says not only do the tares grow alongside the wheat, but also they look just like the wheat. Until they have matured completely, it is impossible to tell one from the other. That is the way things are in the Church. We cannot tell the difference between the genuine and the artificial Christian. The tares in the church dress right, they talk right, they walk right, they give every appearance of being saved. If you examined a real Christian and a tare together, you could not tell. That is why we must never tell someone that they are saved.

- Lesson 3. There was none of the Abundance of Wheat.

So the tares act like wheat, and they look like wheat, but this is where the similarities end. One thing the tare cannot produce is fruit. If you were to open the head of a wheat plant, you would find it filled with wheat kernels.

If you opened the head of the tare, you would find it filled with tiny blade seeds. One thing the tare could never produce was lasting fruit.

So it is with many Christians in the Church. They give all the external appearances of being the real deal. They look right, act right, talk right and walk right but when you get right down to it, there is no fruit in their life.

They lack the fruit of the spirit: which is love, joy, peace patience, kindness, goodness, faithfulness, gentleness, self-control et cetera (Gal 5: 22-23).

<u>Lesson Warning.</u> The parable warns us that eventually there will be the day of harvest when the reapers would be sent into the field to gather the tares first, then the wheat. They will be able to tell the difference between the wheat and the tares by the fruit they produced.

The tares will be burnt. But the wheat will be put in a barn, where it would be processed for human consumption and may be sold for a tidy profit by the farmer.

So the implication is very clear. When this life has run its course, there are only two possible destinations for every human soul. Every human who lives and dies as a tare will find himself cast into the fires of hell, to be eternally separated from the presence of God (1 Thes 1:8-9).

The genuine believer, on the other hand, can look forward to going to heaven to be gathered in the Lord's House in Heaven. (John 14:1-3) The question is: <u>which will it be for you?</u> It will all depend on whether you are a tare (unsaved) or you are a wheat (saved).

Jesus says: He who has ears, let him hear. God has spoken to our hearts this morning. If the Holy Spirit is calling you to come settle your case with God right now, please let nothing stand in your way. Give your life to God today and allow Him to transform you from a <u>tare</u> into a <u>wheat</u> in the name of the Father, Son and Holy Spirit. Amen.

Chapter 7

TEXT: MATTHEW 13:1-9

TOPIC: "WHICH SOIL ARE YOU?"

Greetings and welcome. This sermon is about the parable of the sower as recorded in Matthew 13:1-9.

Introduction. We have all heard about Jesus' parables. Some of the parables are very familiar to us like the Parable of the Sower. But we should not allow that familiarity to close our minds to hearing God speak to us again through His word.

Most of you will have heard a parable described as "an earthly story with a heavenly or spiritual meaning". That is a simple definition of a parable.

A parable is also a comparison of two subjects for the purpose of teaching. It usually proceeds from the known to the unknown in order to teach something spiritual.

A parable holds the attention of the hearers, enables them to see themselves and while dealing with something well known, adds a twist which fascinates and makes the hearer reflect. Why did Jesus teach in parables you may ask?

Well, in verse 1 of Matthew Chapter 13, we see that He has moved from teaching in the Synagogue to teaching in the open air, by the seashore. This move is significant in Matthew's gospel. Having been rejected by the religious leaders of the day, He moves now out into the open air and addresses the crowds of common people. By telling parable, He holds their attention, to fascinate without alienating them. Secondly, if we look at verse 35 of the same Chapter, we will see that parables are an instrument of revelation but only for those to whom it is given to see. The parable revealed truth to those who were hungry to receive it but concealed from those who were too lazy to seek its meaning.

In other wise, as people hear parables they are challenged to see where they stand in relation to the Kingdom of God which Christ brings. This morning, the parable of the sower is our mirror to show us where we stand in relation to the Kingdom of God. Look at yourself in this mirror and find out where you stand.

Our reading says that on the same day Jesus went out of the house and sat by the lake. Such large crowds gathered around him that he got into a boat and sat in it, while all the people stood on the shore. Then he told them "A farmer went out to sow seed. As he was scattering the seed, some fell along the path, and the birds came out and ate it up. Some fell on rocky places, where it did not have much soil. It sprang up quickly, because the soil was shallow. But when the sun came up, the plants were scorched, and they withered because they had no roots.

Other seeds fell among thorns, which grew up and choked the plants. Still other seed fell on good soil, where it produced a crop - a hundred, sixty or thirty times what was sown. He who has ears, let him hear" (Matthew 13:1-9)

In this parable, we see that the farmer sows the seed in the field. The seed which the farmer sows is able to transform the soil. The seed is the <u>Word of God</u> proclaimed by the sower preacher of God.

The Kingdom of God comes when the seed and the soil come together. And the Kingdom comes into a life where the seed takes root and begins to germinate and shoot.

In this parable, we see that there are four soils that the seed falls into:

1. The shallow soil (verses 4)
2. The superficial soil (verses 5-6)
3. The secular soil (verses 7)
4. The successful soil (verses 8)

Each of us in our Christian life belongs to one of these soils but the seed which is God's word is the same. It is the kind of soil we are that determines the fruit we bear when the seed which is the Word of God is sown into our lives.

If the seed is the same then which soil are you?

a) Other seeds fell on rocky ground. The shallow soil is the rocky hard soil with countless feet, hooves of animals and cartwheels travelling over them. Jesus uses the imagery of a hard path which the seed finds impossible to penetrate and hungry birds come to snatch it away as illustration of how some hear the Word of God but do not <u>digest it,</u> <u>understand it,</u> or <u>appropriate it in their lives</u>.

They are very vulnerable to losing it all as the devil comes quickly into such a heart and snatches it all away. Hebrews 4:2 tells us that for the seed to be effectual, it must not only be heard but <u>also combined with faith</u>. The seed planted on to a hard heart that does not receive <u>it with faith</u>, is easily snatched away and bears no fruit at all. Are you this kind of soil? Do you hear the word of God and instantly forget about it?

As Malachi so rightly told his hearers - there comes a time in life when you have to plough up the unploughed ground in order to receive the seed. For some of us here this morning, that is the very challenge we need to hear today.

Our heart is a hard path and though we hear the Word of God, it is so easily snatched away. Even before the end of this sermon, it is gone and we do not remember a thing that was preached. And so day in, day out, we fail to bear good fruit in our lives because our heart is stoney and hard for the seed of the Gospel to penetrate and make a change. Are you this kind of soil?

    b)   The second kind of soil is the superficial soil.

Jesus explains that this type of soil receives the seed which is the Word of God, with great enthusiasm, makes a great start but as soon as trouble or persecution comes, they fall away because there is no root, no depth to their belief. This kind of person can jollied along in the right atmosphere and company but they have no roots to stand on their own and once on their own, they fall away quickly. They will blow with the prevailing wind. They are superficial in their faith. This seed comes to nothing in the life of the hearer and bears no fruit in the world.

Let me humbly say this. There are too many such Christians in Churches. They start off great but soon are blown away with the prevailing wind of the company they are in. They are Christians at Church but not at home or at work.

This seed dies and bears no lasting fruit. Why do you think we can be any different? The challenge to us all here is not to be content with superficial faith or superficial Christianity and not allow others to settle for superficial faith. We must challenge ourselves and encourage others not to settle for what is superficial. That which is superficial never lasts, it quickly withers and dies. Is your Christian faith superficial? Are you the superficial soil?

    c)   <u>The third kind of soil is the secular soil.</u> Verse 7

The seed fell among thorns which grew up and choked the plants. This seed seems to start well. There is growth. There appears to be roots going down into the soil but all is not well. This soil has never been weaned from the secular world around it. It still contains the thorns and thistles of the old worldview and way of life. It is deceptive or delights in the wealth of the world. Such a person is concerned with things of this world, his status and financial standing. These things are the priorities of his life and they slowly take over, grow stronger and choke the shoots of faith. Again this seed comes to nothing in such soil.

Let me ask you seriously this morning. Are you more concerned with labels on your clothing than the label of your character? The seed took root and shoots began to grow but the concerns and cares of this world were more important in this life. We all know that weeds and thorns need to be dug out early before they take root and become persistent problems.

Such thorns are very subtle in life-taking root unseen and then growing to choke the life of faith. Left even for a shorttime they quickly spread and began to take over. The same is true in our lives. We need to be ruthless in digging out the worldview which is not biblical. Unfortunately, we talk so freely and easily of things today that the Bible considers sin. We embrace lifestyles and life choices that are sinful and we think we can embrace them and live as Christians. The truth is that such things choke the life out of our faith and it comes to nothing in our lives. We all know such temporary disciples of Christ are common in churches. Be warned and do not become the secular soil for the Gospel.

    d)   The fourth and last soil is the successful soil.

Verse 8 says still other seed fell on good soil where it produced a crop a hundred, sixty, or thirty times. You know this person is no different than any of the other three soils mentioned before: That is

- The shallow soil
- The superficial soil
- The secular soil

And the seed is scattered in the same way upon the soil of his heart. He hears the exact same word (seed) as the first soil. He hears it with excitement like the second soil. He lives in the exact same world with all its deceits and temptations as the third soil.

The difference is the roots go deep and it produces fruit in due season.

But how did this seed become fruitful?

Jesus said: "Unless a grain of wheat falls in the ground and dies, it remains alone, a single seed. But if it dies, it produces many seeds (John 12:24). There is the answer."

The price of being fruitful is dying to self so that the life of Christ might be seen in and through our lives. The key to good soil prepared for the seed to bear fruit is for the hard ground to be ploughed and broken up. Weeds removed and stones removed. The seed was planted, watered and nourished. Then it can bear fruit. But take notice that the soil cannot do anything by itself. The sower, the pastor does it all. He ploughs up the field. He removes the weeds. He plants the seed and makes it bear fruit. The soil lies barren without those things being done by the sower. It is an ongoing relationship between the soil and the sower that brings the seed to fruition.

It is the same in spiritual life.

An ongoing relationship with Christ brings about spiritual fruit in due season.

This morning, let me remind you that as the pastor of Wesley United Methodist Church, I am the sower. The Lord sent me here to sow the seed which is the word of God in your hearts to bear fruit.

Unfortunately, there are four different soils to deal with: The Shallow, the superficial, the secular, and the successful soil. Which soil describes you and which soil do you want to be?

The seed will always be the same, the sower will always be sent by God but it is the soil that describes us whether we are <u>shallow</u>, <u>superficial</u>, <u>secular</u>, or <u>successful soil</u>. And whether we will bear fruit or not.

The Bible says in Matthew 7:16-19 that "By their fruit you will know them. Do people pick grapes from thorn brushes, or figs from thistles? Likewise every good tree bears good fruit, but a bad tree bears bad fruit. A good tree cannot bear bad fruit, and a bad tree cannot bear good fruit. Every tree that does not bear good fruit is cut down and thrown into the fire".

We are also reminded in Matthew 3:10 that "Even now the ax is laid to the root of the trees. Therefore, every tree which does not bear good fruit is cut down and thrown into the fire.

May this parable of the sower be a mirror for us to see ourselves just as we are and take steps to be fruitful in the Kingdom of God. "Which soil are you?" This morning, may the Lord give us a new heart and put a new spirit within us, and remove the heart of stone from our flesh and give us a heart of flesh to bear good fruit in our lives. "He who has ears, let him hear". In the name of Father, the Son, and the Holy Spirit. Amen.

Chapter 8

TEXT: MATTHEW 10:1-8

TOPIC: "CALLED TO CONFRONT AN EVIL WORLD."

Introduction:

Brothers and Sisters in Christ, greetings in the name of our Lord and Savior Jesus Christ.

This morning, our attention is drawn to the Gospel of Matthew 10:1-8. It is about the mission of the twelve disciples.

It is about Jesus sending them out to make discipleship. Discipleship in the Christian life, is the process of making someone become like Christ in everything.

The primary focus of Jesus coming to the world was to establish the Kingdom of God through His death on the cross.

To be a disciple, therefore, is to follow Christ, learn from Him, believe in Him and serve Him in the Kingdom of God.

Our reading in Matthew 10:1-8, tells us that "Jesus called to him his twelve disciples and gave them authority over unclean spirits, to cast them out, and to heal every disease and every infirmity"

Additionally, He tells them: "proclaim as you go saying: The Kingdom of heaven is at hand; Heal the sick, raise the dead, cleanse lepers, cast out demons. You received without paying; give without pay" (Matthew 10:7-8).

These were the instructions Jesus gave to the twelve disciples when he called them and sent them out two by two. We notice that he did not send them out to preach the gospel without giving them power and authority over demons and diseases. The church cannot witness the world without power. Therefore, He gave them power to drive out evil spirits and to heal every disease and sickness. In other words, they were going out to confront an evil world with the Gospel of Jesus Christ.

While sending them out, Jesus acknowledges the reality of evil in this world. He called his disciples to distinguish between the satanic forces who are enemies of those who belong to the Kingdom of God, and a lost humanity that may be hostile to our efforts but are not our enemy.

If the disciples can begin to see the world as Jesus sees it, looking out on lost humanity through the Lord's eyes and with a heart of compassion, they also will begin to see that they themselves were called to go out and warn the lost world of the coming harvest of judgement, and to invite them into the Lord's kingdom.

Today, we also as disciples of Jesus Christ, are asked to do the same. We are to go out and preach, witness and teach the world about the good news of the Kingdom of God. And there is an urgency to this matter.

This world is not a place of positive direction and affirmation. There is always lurking behind some outward tolerance, real evil. Jesus demands that we not remain silent or impotent in the face of evil. Every disciple of

Jesus is called upon to confront this evil world through the power of the Holy Spirit. And Jesus shows us how to do so. We are to do so by presenting a clear message: "And as you go, say the Kingdom of Heaven is at hand" (Matt 10:7).

It is said that Satan's surest way of making the gospel impotent is simply to keep it from being understood. When we cloud the gospel with political, cultural, social, economic, environmental, ecclesiastical and other such causes, its message is muddled and its power is diluted.

So to confront this evil world, we must be ready to proclaim the realities of the gospel in every sphere that we travel. The world is not our home and Jesus wants us to be itinerant missionaries. Our commitment is needed and our message must be simply: "The kingdom of heaven is at hand". So what do we mean by the Kingdom of God?

In scriptures, the Kingdom of God/ Heaven can be used in three aspects:

1. It is manifested in conversion, when a person enters the sovereign rule of God by trusting in Christ for Salvation. (Matt 18:3)
2. It is manifested in consecration as believers live out the divine principles of God's revelation by obedience to His word. For the kingdom of God is not a matter of eating and drinking, but of righteousness, peace and joy in the Holy Spirit. (Romans 14:17)
3. The kingdom of God will be seen in its glorious consummation when Christ returns to earth to establish and rule it in person and then set-up His eternal kingdom (Matt 25:31)

Although the disciples did not understand it yet, it began with the incarnation of Christ the Messiah and will be consummated at the second coming of Christ.

So what is the message that brings us into this Kingdom? When it comes to the message, it is about repentance and forgiveness manifested in healing the sick, raising the dead, cleansing those who have leprosy and driving out demons.

Jesus wants us to understand that a life of sin that Satan encourages and human depravity wants, is the ultimate bait and switch. Sin promises fulfillment but ultimately brings destruction. Only holy life begun with repentance of sin brings refreshment, forgiveness, healing and restoration.

So we cannot live in holiness and be disciples of Jesus if we hold grudges against each other in the Church, if we do not speak in love to one another, if we are hypocritical liars and constantly show behavior that contradicts what we claim to believe or feel.

The personal and societal destruction that we see all around us, will one day be reversed, and restored to the condition that God intended, when Christ comes again to fulfill His kingdom.

And until the message of God's sovereign provision for man's salvation is clearly understood, accepted and obeyed, trying to apply it to any other area of life is both disobedience to Christ command and futile. The gospel transforms society only as it transforms individuals. Therefore, without transformation in our lives, we cannot transform others.

So the question for us is: Have we been born again into the Kingdom of God? Have we been transformed in our daily lives into truly the image of the people of God? And if we are truly disciples of Jesus Christ, do we have the knowledge and the power of the Holy Spirit to change lives, to win souls, to encounter the evil of the world with the gospel of peace or are we part of the problem?

Jesus says "The harvest is plentiful, but the laborers are few; pray therefore the Lord of the harvest to send out laborers into his harvest" (Matt 9: 37-38).

It is not enough for us to call ourselves Christians and not engage in the battle to win souls for Christ and for the Kingdom of God. The disciples were sent out and we too need to be sent out. For the word of God says: The fruit of the righteous is a tree of life, and he that winneth soul is wise". (Proverbs 11:30)

In Daniel 12:3, we read:

"And they that be wise shall shine as the brightness of the firmament, and they shall turn many to righteousness as the stars forever and ever."

So how do we become successful soul winners? How can we witness the non-believer and bring him or her to Christ? Jesus sets the example for us. When we look at Jesus, his chief trait was his compassion. Compassion is what impelled him in all of his actions. The literary meaning of the word compassion is "to suffer with". When we feel compassion towards someone, we sense the pain and hardship they are experiencing. It is like we are putting ourselves in their shoes. Their trial becomes our trial. Their suffering becomes our suffering.

Matthew 9:35-38 describes Jesus going about his ministries. He is travelling from town to town. Everywhere he goes, he teaches in the synagogues. And healing was a big part of His ministry too. He healed every disease and infirmity. When he gazed out at the people gathered about him, he was filled with compassion. Their pain, their loneliness, their grief, all became his. His response to their plight was loving compassion.

There is no doubt that the backbone of Jesus' mission was compassion.

It was compassion that compelled Him to take on our human flesh in the first place. And compassion prompted him to pour out himself to death on the cross. In view of this, we who are disciples of Jesus Christ must also be compelled to be of the same mind as Christ. We must exhibit compassion in our lives.

Throughout every generation, compassion has been the calling of the church.

The Church - the "people of God", "the body of Christ", the "New Creation", the fellowship of Faith" exists purposely for Christ's sake and as members, compassion becomes our chief endeavor. The task for us is: do we have compassion towards one another at Wesley United Methodist Church? When was the last time we showed compassion to a member of our church? By calling to check on them, to pray for them, to give them a word of encouragement, to bless them with our resources, to help them deal with issues in their lives?

Do not tell me it is the duty of the pastor only. No. We all have been called to be disciples of Jesus Christ. That means not only do we participate in the life activities of the Church, but also we are commanded to be disciples of Christ which include showing compassion to all members of the Church and the community, loving them, bearing their burdens with them, praying for them, showing them love and loving them for who they are. If we are not doing this, then we need to examine our role in the Church. From generation to generation, the Church has continued to respond to times of need with a servant's heart. We find ourselves in the middle of such a time with the Covid 19 outbreak. Compassion calls us to respond with a servant's heart. Today, we see examples of servant hearts all around us.

We see,

- Medical workers who tirelessly treat patients
- Researchers works up towards treatment and vaccines
- Governors of each state are working to do whatever is in their powers to keep the public safe.
- Truckers who ship vital goods from place to place.
- Factory workers willing to work extra shifts in order to meet demand for goods
- Volunteers reaching out to feed the hungry and help the vulnerable
- And everyone follows practices to curtail the spread of the virus.

And thank God that we have members in our Church who are doing all these things to bring glory to God.

But that is not enough. We must also bring the Gospel of salvation to all for "Man does not live by bread alone but by every word that proceeds from the mouth of God" (Matthew 4:4).

The Gospel of salvation is very urgent for the world. Its evil representatives oppress the poor and needy, commit robbery, does not restore a pledge (Ezekiel 18: 12), persecute the poor, (Psalm 10: 2), puts heavy burden on them and defrauds them (Amos 5:11), grinds them down (Isaiah 3:15), and devour them (Habakkuk 3:14).

Indeed, the world has little use for the afflicted and false prophets have no mercy or compassion but rather use and abuse people for their own selfish advantage.

But we who are the Christians, we who are the body of Christ, we are called to have compassion and to reach out with the message of hope and salvation.

Christians who have little compassion for the poor, the sick, and the afflicted, are ineffective and inconsistent representatives of Jesus Christ despite their sound knowledge of the Word of God and their high morals. Such people lack an important credential that makes them the servant of Christ.

III. So we cannot confront the evil world if our message is not clear and our credentials as Christians are fake. Christ commands us to "Heal the sick, raise the dead, cleanse those who have leprosy, drive out demons" (Matt 10:8).

Doctors, lawyers, and other professionals prominently display their diplomas and other documents that certify their qualifications and authority to practice.

In a far more important way, those of us who represent Christ must have credentials that confirm our divine mission and message.

In the Gospel of Matthew, Jesus gave confirming signs for His own ministry, and now He calls the apostles to demonstrate their authority by performing works confirming their message. The signs of a true apostle are "signs and wonders and miracles". It was with those evidential signs that

Jesus empowered the apostles as He sent them out on their first mission to preach to the lost sheep of the house of Israel.

The question then is,

Do we have the credentials today needed to fulfil the mission of the Church?

Truly, I tell you. We cannot make disciples without showing compassion and without power to back us up.

Our church therefore needs the outpouring of the Holy Spirit upon us and we need all the gifts of the Holy Spirit to fulfill our mission. That means first, we must all search our hearts and minds, and see if we have strayed from the Word of God and repent of our sins and ask for restoration into the Kingdom of God. We must see if we have offended a church member in any way, repent and ask for forgiveness, reconcile and love one another.

As a Church, we cannot confront the evils of the world if we are part of the problem, if we ourselves dabble in sin. Only the redeemed can do so.

For the world is truly sick of sin. Only the proclamation of the Gospel by righteous people can bring deliverance.

In a spiritual sense, sin is a sickness that the message of the gospel cures.

Those dead in trespass and sins are raised to life through the Gospel.

Those who are spiritually unclean, represented by lepers, can be cleansed and made spiritually whole by the gospel.

Those under the dominion of Satan, and the demonic, can enter the Kingdom of God through the Gospel.

Even now, God is demonstrating His sympathetic heart to those who are suffering, those who are hurting, the afflicted and the needy. Even now, he is touching the sick among us and bringing healing. Even now, he is delivering us from the bondage of sins, oppression and death in the name of Jesus. Even now, he is setting free those who are bound in chains and imprisoned in bondage. Jesus is still working in the world to transform lives. And he needs labourers. He needs you. He needs me. Help is wanted. And Jesus is accepting applications. He needs you now. He reminds us and encourages us "to work the works of him that sent us, while it is day; the night cometh when no man can work" (John 9:4)

Conclusion: So, the future of Wesley United Methodist Church, and its effectiveness in fulfilling the mission of the Church depend on us. Our challenge is to be true disciples of Jesus Christ. We must be compassionate, we must share the good news, we must demonstrate the love of God in our hearts to each other and love all believers, love the poor, the sick, the weak, the troubled, the marginalized, and the downtrodden.

Like the disciples, sent by Jesus to win souls, we too must win souls for Christ. We can do it by the grace and power of the Holy Spirit.

May the Lord God Almighty grant us His grace, mercy, love and guidance to work together to fulfill the mission of the Church: "To make disciples of Jesus Christ for the transformation of the world" in the name of the Father, and of the Son and of the Holy Spirit. Amen.

Chapter 9

TEXT: PSALM 6:1-10

TOPIC: "FINDING REST IN JESUS"

<u>Introduction</u>: We all get exhausted, weary, stressed and lack peace in this life at one time or another. It is clear that these days, stress is a common problem in modern life. There is no doubt that every individual will experience stress in one way or the other.

Stress is defined as "an internal state which can be caused by physical demands of the body or by environmental and social situations, which is evaluated as potentially harmful, uncontrollable, or exceeding our resources for coping".

In our passage of scripture, Psalm 6:1-10, we find David in a sleepless night. In the first seven verses of the Psalm, David is troubled, terrified, faint and weak. He was simply trying to say that he was worn out from <u>groaning</u>, <u>tossing</u>, <u>turning</u>, and <u>weeping</u> through the night.

You can feel his agony in the painful question he asks in O, Lord "How long?". It is a cry of a man who has hung on, and held out, but he is growing tired. He is about ready to raise the white flag of surrender. He is about to give up. He is simply worn out.

Now, let me ask you a question. Am I speaking to anyone that is tired? You may say Pastor, "I am not tired: I am sick and tired". Others of you may say "I am sick of being tired". The truth is you are just worn out. Worn out at home, at work and at church.

For so many of us this whole Covid-19 issue has just been so very exhausting. Mentally, we are tired of getting our arms around this new normal.

Emotionally, we are trying hard to live life, juggle our responsibilities, and be faithful to God.

And so now, into the 12th or 14th week of the Corona Virus, some of us are starting to crumble. And as the pieces fall, so do we, and we are not even sure what happened.

We just know that we are spent, dry, <u>weary</u>, and totally exhausted in every way we can be. So what do we do when we find ourselves simply worn out?

In Mark 6:31-32, Jesus said to His disciples, "Come ye yourselves apart into a desert place, and rest a while; for there were many coming and going; and they had no leisure so much as to eat. And they departed into the desert by ship privately".

This is a must for every Christian. If you do not come apart, you will come apart. If you are worn out today, I want you to step into this passage of Scripture with me, and let us find wisdom and strength in the Word of God to take a rest.

Well, what was bothering David? He was run down <u>mentally</u>, <u>emotionally</u>, <u>physically</u>, and <u>spiritually</u>. David was just like you and me. His body was simply tired. He was damned worn out. In another Psalm, David says "My strength is dried up like a potsherd" - That is like a piece of pottery that has been in fire so long that it is hard and dry. So what causes this problem of reduced strength and stress? What makes us tired?

There are five:

1. <u>The Demand of Service:</u> can break us down. When you serve the Lord, it will take strength from you. Some days, even the best of leaders of faith filled believers, can grow weary and exhausted. When you have a job, you can get exhausted. All of us are humans and we are going to get tired. You can get tired no matter who you are; whether in the Church or on your job.
2. <u>The Disability of sickness</u>: can get you tired. David wrote this psalm after he had recovered from an illness which threatened to prove fatal. You know, sometimes, we just get sick. Have you noticed how a simple sinus infection can shut down your entire body? When you get sick, you do not feel like doing anything. You don't even feel like eating. You are just there and you do not want to move. You do not feel spiritual. Your strength has gone on you. Sickness has taken that from you. It causes reduced strength and stress and makes you tired and weak.
3. <u>The Damage of Sin</u>: can sap your strength and stress. No doubt, David is consumed in thought with his pay day for a half an hour's worth of sin when he had committed adultery, and tried to cover it up with murder.

He says "For my life is spent with grief, and my eyes with sighing; my strength faileth because of mine iniquity and my bones are consumed." (Psalm 31:10).

Notice that unresolved guilt will sap strength out of our lives. There is nothing that will cause you to sleep better than to know there is nothing between your soul and the savior.

4. <u>The Devastation of Sorrow</u>: In verse 6 of Psalm 6 we read: "I am weary with moaning; every night I flood my bed with tears; I drench my couch with my weeping." What a moving description of a broken and contrite heart?

Not only was David broken by conviction gripping his soul, but he was tearful at many losses in his life. He had lost his best friend Jonathan, and a new born baby son, and a daughter that had been molested by her brother.

If you have ever had a loved one to fall deadly sick or to pass away, and most of us have, you know that being in great anguish and sorrow just absolutely pulls the strength out of you. 1 Samuel 30: 4 says: "Then David and the people that were with him lifted up their voice and wept, until they had no more power to weep. Sorrow and death can sap our strength and devaste us.

5. <u>The Device of Satan</u>. Can sap your strength. Verse 7 of Psalm 6 says: My eyes waste away because of grief, it grows weak because of all my foes". The devil is a master strategist, and the devil knows exactly when to move in on you and to attack you. You see, the devil does not fight fair.

The story is told in Deuteronomy 25:17-18, Amalek was a wicked, canaanite king and here is what God said to Moses: "Remember what Amalek did unto thee by the way, when you were come forth out of Egypt, how he met thee by the way, and smote the hindmost of thee, even all that were feeble behind thee, when thou was faint and weary, and he feared not God".

This satanically inspired enemy said, "I am not going to attack the strong ones; I am going to find those who are hobbling and weak, some older men, some older women, some child. Those are the ones I am going to attack." Satan sees the advantage over us. But again, Satan is no respecter of moments. He may move in during low tide spiritually or he may move in after a great spiritual victory.

David has gone from despair in his circumstances to despairing for his life. He is not only losing sleep, but he is losing interest in life.

Satan's method is to use small, daily irritations of people, pressures and problems to tap against our soul until we give in or give up.

During the Last Supper, Jesus told Peter in Luke 22:31, "Simon, Simon, behold Satan hath desired to have you, that he may sift you as wheat".

Peter's response in this sifting reveals a similar pattern in our lives. What are the warning signs of a life being worn out?

They are:

Our praying becomes silenced.

Our performance becomes spirit-less

Our profession becomes secretive and we become more vulnerable to the attacks of Satan. That is why more of us should be praying, fasting and studying the Word of God. Unless we want to be attacked by Satan.

So we can get tired because of

1. The demand for work
2. By sickness
3. By sinning
4. By sorrow
5. By the devices of Satan

But thank God. We can renew our strength.

Isaiah 40:31 says "But they that wait upon the Lord shall renew their strength; they shall run and not be weary; and they shall walk and not faint".

Jesus has promised us rest.

In Matthew 11:28, he says "Come unto me, all ye that labour and are heavy laden, and I will give you rest" <u>if you are tired, worn out and broken in spirit</u>.

The truth is that you probably don't need to see a psychiatrist, doctor, or a minister. You probably just need a rest.

That may be all that is wrong with you. You just need to rest.

Genesis 2:2 reminds us "And on the seventh day God ended His work which He had made; and he rested on the seventh day from all His work which He had made".

God may not always give us what we want, but He gives us what we need.

Listen Brothers and Sisters. God knows there is a time to work. But God also knows that you need rest. He took Elijah off to a little spiritual retreat up in the caves, and fed him with angel food cake, and He just let him rest.

Jesus also took his disciples and got away from the crowds into the mountains to rest. The question is: What are you doing to give yourself a rest?

Psalm 127:2 says "It is vain for you to rise up early, to sit up late, to eat the bread of sorrows; for so she giveth his beloved sleep". He is saying that it is vain to not get your rest.

And one of the sure tests of our having been renewed with rest is the peace of mind which follows.

Peace does not mean a retreat from the world, but rather a serenity which comes and remains though the outside world may be in turmoil. And when you know that God has got the whole world in His hand and your little world under control, you can say with the psalmist in Psalm 4:8, "I will both lay me down in peace, and sleep; for thou, Lord only makest me dwell in safety."

The question for us today is: Are you taking a good rest? Or are you overworking yourself? Are you under stress? Are you worn out and broken in spirit? Have your trials and temptations? Is there trouble anywhere? Are we weak and heavyladen? Are cumbered with a load of care? Well, you must take it to Jesus and you will find solace there.

Christians who have run away from God in their hurry and rush for worldly things need to stop and catch up on spiritual things. May the Lord help us find true rest in Jesus in the name of the Father, Son and the Holy Spirit. Amen.

Chapter 10

TEXT: MATTHEW 28:16-20

TOPIC: "THE GREAT COMMISSION "THE WAY OF FAITH"

INTRODUCTION:

Greetings in the name of our Lord and Savior Jesus the Christ. Today is Trinity Sunday and our text for reflection is taken from Matthew 28: 16-20 tilled "The Great Commission"

It is the last order that Jesus gave to his disciples before He ascended to Heaven. It is Jesus' last word to his disciples. It was a command, an imperative, he says "All authority in heaven and on earth has been given to me. Therefore, go and make disciples of all nations, baptizing them in the name of the Father and of the Son and of the Holy Spirit, and teaching them to obey everything, I have commanded you. And surely I am with you always, to the very end of the age" (Matthew 28:18-20).

The various Gospels emphasize different aspects of this Great Commission. Luke limits Jesus' resurrection appearances to Jerusalem and emphasizes repentance and forgiveness of Sin (Luke 24:46-48).

In Acts 1:8, Luke recounts Jesus' promise of power and the command to "go to the uttermost parts of the earth".

In the Gospel of John, Jesus gives the disciples power to forgive sins (John 20:23).

But when we come to the Gospel of Matthew, we see that from the beginning he emphasized Jesus' teachings. In Matthew 28, Matthew portrays Jesus' last act of ministry as teaching his disciples Christian ministry which involves <u>going</u>, <u>baptizing</u>, making disciples and teaching. In short, the text stamps Jesus' approval on baptism as key element of discipleship and makes baptism norminative for Christians.

It also gives the trinitarian formula "in the name of the Father and of the Son and of the Holy Spirit" that the Church has followed through the centuries.

From generation to generation since the Church was born on the Day of the Pentecost, this Great Commission has stood for ages and it still stands today, as the Church's call to arms.

To understand and appreciate the meaning of the Great Commission and to take Jesus' last command seriously, we need to know the nature and mission of the Church.

The church's identity, its mission, and its future is grounded primarily in the Bible. In the New Testament, there are more than eighty images of the Church by a conservative estimate.

However, four images dominate the New Testament's description of the Church: The Church is "<u>the people of God</u>", "<u>the new creation</u>", "<u>the fellowship in faith</u>", and the "<u>body of Christ</u>".

First, in 1 Peter 2:9 we read: As the people of God", the Church is set in the story of God dealing with the chosen people. "You are a chosen race, a royal priesthood, a holy nation, God's own people, in order that you may proclaim the mighty acts of him who called you out of darkness into his marvelous light"

The church is in a long tradition as the Law and the Prophets and shares the same heritage and mission as the "Israel of God" (Gal 6: 15-16). The church is a holy nation rooted in a covenantal relationship with God and set apart for special purposes.

It is "Abraham's offspring" (Gal 3:29) and as such the Church shares in Abraham's posterity. The original covenant in Abraham's posterity. The original covenant with and promise to Abraham was that he was to be a means by which God blessed all families of the earth. (Genesis 12: 2-3).

Therefore, the existence of the people of God, the Church, is due to God's own initiative, not the <u>merits</u> or <u>power</u> or <u>prestige</u> of the people. It is by God's grace that the Church, "the people of God", are <u>created</u>, <u>called</u>, <u>sustained</u>, <u>judged</u>, and saved (Romans 9:19-33).

The church is also viewed as the <u>Flock</u>, God's flock with Jesus as the Shepherd (Hebrews 13: 20). In Luke 12:32, we read "Do not be afraid, little flock, for it is your Father's good pleasure to give you the kingdom".

The flock owes its existence to the Shepherd who calls each sheep by name, seeks them when they go astray, and guides them into the fold. Christ is the Good Shepherd, who seeks to bring other sheep into the same fold (John 10:16), who cares for the sheep who have no shepherd (Mark 6:34), and who gathers lost sheep (Matthew 10:6, 15:24).

Thus, there is a strong interdependence between the flock and the shepherd, and the relationship is characterized by trust and compassion.

<u>A second dominant image of the Church in the New Testament is the "New Creation".</u>

As the images of the "people of God" set the Church in the context of the covenant history of Israel, the images of the "New Creation" set the church in a universal or cosmic context.

The same God who acts within a particular covenant history also acts within the whole human family and all of creation.

God's purpose in choosing a particular people is to accomplish universal and cosmic purposes.

The Church, therefore, is composed of those who live as a "new creation". The Bible says: "If anyone is in Christ, there is a "new creation", everything old has passed away; see everything has become new!" (2 Cor 5:17).

Christ represents a "New Creation", the first fruits of a new humanity (1 Cor 15: 20-23).

The Holy Spirit is at work within the Christian Community as a guarantee of the coming redemption of the creation (Rom 8: 23).

Another way of talking about the "New creation" is in terms of the "kingdom of God"

In the New testament, the kingdom of God was understood as the opposite of the Kingdom of Satan.

Now, persons must make a radical choice between the two Kingdoms, which continue to struggle for dominance.

Those who inherit the kingdom of God have a special place within it. It includes the despised, the poor, the weak, the hungry, the persecuted; but they become rich and blessed, beloved and joyful, as they share in the reign of God (Matthew 5: 3-10, 22: 1-10).

<u>The third dominant images</u> of the church is "The Fellowship of Faith". It is the fellowship of saints, those who are sanctified in Christ Jesus (1 Cor

1:2). As the company of saints, the church depends on the ongoing activity of God. It is God's holiness that the Church shares (Heb 12:10)

Because the One who called the Church into being is holy, the Church must be holy (1 Peter 1:15-16). The Church's holiness or sanctification, is related to Christ's sacrificial death. "We have been sanctified through the offering of the body of Jesus Christ once and for all" (Heb 10: 10, 14, 29). When the Church is spoken of as the Saints, the power of the Holy Spirit is assumed to be at work within it. The community has been <u>born of the spirit</u> and <u>baptized into one spirit</u>. The spirit is <u>poured out on the community</u> and the <u>spirit dwells within it</u>.

In the light of this, the believers who make up the church are bound together by a new boldness (Acts 4:10-2), a unanimity of praise and prayer (Acts 4:23-31), a transformation in the idea of property and concern for others needs (Acts 2:44-45), a new mutuality and hospitality (Rom 14:3). The believers treat every person as one for whom Christ died, and accordingly avoid any action that would injure another (Rom 14:13-15).

They give priority to the common good and to God's work in building up the household of faith rather than to self-esteem and self-interest. They help to bear the burden of those who are weak in the faith (Rom 15:1-3).

Above all, they live in such harmony with one another that their life together glorifies God. (Romans 15:6).

Lastly, the dominant image of the Church in the New Testament is the "body of Christ". This image is found explicitly in Paul's Letters. The meaning of the image varies and it is difficult, if not impossible, to reduce it to one definition. When Paul refers to the Church as the "body of Christ" it is understood that he uses the image as a way of conveying the truth that all the gifts of the Holy Spirit are activated by one and the same spirit, who allots to each one individually just as the spirit-chooses (1 Cor 12:11).

It is also understood that all have been baptized into one body and this baptism has destroyed the old solidarities of race, class, and ranking. It is an incorporation into a body of interdependent members and mutual sharing of the Spirit's variety of gifts.

Just as the body is one and has many members, and all the members of the body, though many, are one body, so it is with Christ. (1 Cor 12:12).

The imagery of the body makes clear that Christ is the head of the Church. "In Him the whole fullness of deity dwells bodily, and you have come to fullness in him, who is the head of every ruler and authority" (Col 2: 9-10)

Now, with this understanding the question is: "Does this picture or imagery of the Church truly reflect the life of Wesley United Methodist Church?"

Unfortunately, while some of our members are striving to become Christ-like, to live according to the Word of God and to obey God in all things. others continue to dabble in Christianity and other religions without committing their lives to the Lord Jesus Christ for total transformation through forgiveness of sin and the baptism of the Holy Spirit.

Those have become the bane of the Church causing great distress, division, annoyance and strife in the body of Christ. We pray that God will have mercy on us and snatch such people from the powers of evil, vanity, self-righteousness and bring them to the knowledge of salvation through faith in Jesus Christ our Lord. For the Bible warns "Not everyone who says "Lord, Lord, shall enter into the Kingdom of Heaven, but he who does the will of my Father who is in heaven." (Matt 7:21).

So with our understanding of the nature and mission of the Church, as "the People of God", the "Fellowship of Faith", the Body of Christ, and the "New Creation", the Great Commission becomes our marching orders and paramount assignment from Jesus for the growth and development of the Church.

In the great commission, we are first commanded to "Go". To do so, we must, as a church, be proactive. It is not enough for us to sit back and enjoy our relationship with God and each other, while souls are perishing everyday in our society.

We are commanded to take the initiative and make the first move. And so when we see someone sitting near us on Sunday at Church that we do not know, let us introduce ourselves and offer a word of welcome.

Unfortunately, oftentimes there are members of the Church who exhibit attitudes and characteristics that are not Christlike to other members against the command of Jesus that we must love one another. Such people need to think twice, repent and take steps to reconcile with one another as part of our obedience to Christ.

There is no place in the life of the Church for the Spirit of dissension, enmity, strife, hatred, jealousy and anger. That is evil and demonic. Christ commands us to obey His commands. "If you love me you will obey my command". And this is my commandment that ye love one another" (John 13:34).

We cannot take the Great Commission seriously if we cannot live peacefully in the Church. Christ warns us in Matthew 12:30 "He that is not with me is against me, and that gathers not with me scatters abroad".

We must therefore be careful not to scatter what God has gathered into the Church by His grace and mercy.

And so in between Sunday mornings, take it upon yourself to introduce yourself to those joining your club, association, those at your workplace and be the first to welcome and invite them to visit your church. When you do, you will be taking the Great Commission seriously.

Secondly, we are commanded to make disciples.

Making disciples should be put in the right perspective. Jesus did not say we should go and recruit church members. Church members are not recruited. They are discipled. The church does not need to have its roll filled with members who are not committed to the Lord Jesus Christ. Who will not come to Church, to worship, participate in prayer, bible study and the life of the Church. The implication is that disciples are made, not born. God may call us from birth to be his Children, but someone has to give us the training to be disciples. And the best way to make disciples is to discipline ourselves and then share those disciplines with others. A disciple, therefore, is one who is disciplined, who conforms to the standards and expectations of his teacher. As disciples of Jesus Christ, we are disciplined by his teachings and example. We cannot therefore make disciples if we do not practice what the Bible teaches us. We can only teach what we know and what we believe and practice.

To be successful therefore in making disciples, we must start by strengthening our own spiritual disciplines through prayer, fasting, bible study, giving and service. Then share with others by taking time to explain to others what we believe, what we do and why.

Every church member and church leader needs to be born again by water and by the Holy Spirit in order to carry out the Great Commission. In addition, each of us who are part of the "Body of Christ" must know why we go to Church and be able to explain it to those who do not know.

As believers, we go to Church to praise God and listen for God's word, not to be entertained. We got to study the scrip-

ture to find meaning and direction for our lives, not to socialize with friends. We got to seek to be a blessing to others not because we have to, but because we are grateful for the many ways God has blessed us. We go to pray and thank God for His mercies and ask God to be with those in need.

And when trouble comes, we look to God for comfort and strength.

In times of uncertainty, we are not afraid because we know that God is with us, we are not alone, His grace is sufficient for every need.

We go to Church because we believe that all things work together for good for those who love the Lord and are called according to his purposes (Roman 8:28).

And lastly, we go to Church because we believe that nothing shall separate us from the love of God in Christ Jesus our Lord.

Thirdly, we are commanded <u>to share the Good News</u>.

The Gospel of Jesus Christ is inclusive. It is not just for us, but for everyone who calls upon the name of the Lord. "For everyone who calls on the name of the Lord shall be saved" (Rom 10:13).

The question is: Are we willing to go and make disciples of our neighborhood across the street and across town where we work even though people may be different?

Well, Jesus commands us to go make disciples of all the nations. We may not be able to travel to other countries to make disciples but we can make a lot of disciples in our own backyards - just where we are. All we need is to be proactive and take the initiative and make the first move.

We need to have the willingness to embrace those who are different, letting the love of Christ alone be the tie that binds us together as one.

Let us not just sit in our homes and Church and think people will come to join us in Church to worship God. We must go and make disciples. Jesus says:

"But you will receive power when the Holy Spirit comes on you, and you will be my witnesses in Jerusalem, and in all Judea and Samaria, and to the ends of the earth" (Acts 1:8).

Are you ready to follow His call this morning?

Chapter 11

TEXT: JOHN 14:15-21

TOPIC: "WE NEED THE HOLY SPIRIT"

Introduction

Today, we are drawing near the end of this season of Easter.

On Thursday May 21, 2020, we will celebrate the Ascension - the physical departure of Christ from Earth into the presence of God in Heaven. And next Sunday May 31, will be Pentecost, the birth of the Church.

But today, it is still Easter, the Season we have been learning what it means to follow the risen Christ.

Throughout this Eastertide, we have been examining what it means to be a disciple - a follower of Jesus or how discipleship looks like through sermons I have preached so far.

In those sermons, we experienced an awakening in our lives.

Thomas awakened us to the realization that doubt is a necessary element of real faith. We learned that as disciples of Jesus, we need to be together, to break bread together and to examine God's word together.

We also learned that Jesus awakened us to recognize him as the Gate of Salvation (John 10:9) "I am the gate; whoever enters through me will be saved! Above all, we learned, as we witness Jesus and His disciple in the Upper Room for the last supper, that following Jesus means surrendering ourselves completely to him, just as he surrendered himself completely to the Father's will, and for the Father's glory.

Each of these lessons highlights a different element of discipleship. We need to pay attention to:

1. That followers of Jesus experience doubt. And they ask hard questions.
2. That followers of Jesus stay connected to the community of faith, depending on one another for encouragement and accountability.
3. That followers of Jesus listen for His voice, and follow Christ into the fold for safety and out into the world.
4. That followers of Jesus surrender themselves to lives of service and humility, to bring glory to God alone.

These are all important elements of discipleship that each one of us needs to grasp and understand in order to play our roles accordingly in the Church. But that is not all.

Today, we will examine one more. And really, all the others are bound up in this one - the promise of the Holy Spirit to us.

On our rest day today, in John 14: 15-21, Jesus is talking to his disciples on the night of His betrayal. He has been talking about being betrayed; being put to death. He has been talking to them that He is going away and where he is going they can-

not come right now. And they do not understand Him. They cannot comprehend the delay of establishing the Kingdom.

In their minds, Jesus is still going to set up the Kingdom almost immediately.

When Jesus talks about death, it troubles them. And so at the beginning of this chapter John 14, He said "Let not your hearts be troubled" For they were indeed troubled.

You see Jesus had been a real defense for the disciples against the Scribes, Pharisees and the religious leaders who attack them everyday. Now what will they do without Jesus' presence?

So Jesus says to them:

"If you love me, you will keep my commandments And I will ask the Father, and He will give you another Advocate, to be with you forever. This is the Spirit of Truth, whom the world cannot receive because it neither sees him nor knows him. You know him, because he abides with you, and he will be in you.

I will not leave you as orphans; I will come to you. Before long, the world will not see me anymore, but you will see me. Because I live, you will also live" (John 14: 15-19).

While these verses are clear that Jesus intends them to comfort them, it is also clear that they issue a challenge to his followers.

By this statement, Jesus calls his disciples into a deeper understanding of what it means to follow him, even after he is no longer physically present.

So the challenge to his disciples, to us is how can we keep following Jesus after he is no longer physically present among us?

The answer is simple and extremely difficult at the same time.

Jesus says: "If you love me, you will keep my commandments" (John 14:15).

But what are those <u>commandments exactly?</u>

In John 13:34, Jesus says: "Love on another, <u>as I have loved you</u>".

And that part "as I have loved you" gets us every time. How on earth are we supposed to be able to love the way Christ loves us? What does that kind of love even look like?

It is interesting to know that in the Greek vocabulary, there are no less than six Greek words we translate in English as "love". The word we find in this passage is repeated at least four times in John 15:21 alone. It is the word "Agape".

The passage reads: "Whoever has my commands and obeys them, he is the one who <u>loves</u> (agape) me. He who <u>loves</u> (agape) me, will be <u>loved</u> (agape) by my Father, and I too will <u>love</u> (agape) him and show myself to him" (John 15:21).

Agape is the most radical version of love expressed in Greek. This selfless love was extended to everyone, from family members to total strangers. It is referred to as a "gift love, the highest form of Christian love".

It is a self-giving, indiscriminate love that Jesus demonstrated to his disciples when he knelt down and washed their feet (John 13:1-17), the kind of love he showed on the cross. It is the kind of indiscriminate, selfless love he offers to us, and commands us to offer to each other.

It is a tall order. Jesus knows this.

That is why he tells us that we will have some help. He says "I will ask the Father to give you another advocate, to be with you forever" (John 14:16). That advocate is the Holy Spirit, the spirit of Christ, the Spirit of Truth, the Spirit of Glory, the Comforter, the Paraclete (Greek).

The Holy Spirit is the Advocate who brings the truth of that love and life to people in this time after Easter, which makes faith possible.

Just as Jesus is our Advocate before the father, the Holy Spirit is our Advocate before the world. And we need Him badly because the world does not recognize Jesus as Christ, and because of this, the world cannot see the spirit of truth.

On the night before the crucifixion, Pilate asked Jesus, "What is truth?" (John 18: 38), and Jesus did not say a word. He did not need to.

The answer was standing right in front of Pilate.

Jesus had earlier that evening told Thomas "I am the Way, and the Truth and the Life" (John 14:6). And now Jesus says that the world "neither sees the spirit of Truth nor knows him. But you know him, because he abides with you, and he will be in you" (John 14:17).

So the question for us is: Do we have the Holy Spirit? Have we experienced Him in our life? Are we walking in the Spirit of Truth, are we obedient to His guidance, teachings and leadership? As individuals and as Church?

Scripture teachers that the Holy Spirit is an extension of God's personality. He is the third person of the Godhead Trinity. It is imperative therefore, for every believer in Christ to have the Holy Spirit.

Roman 8:9 says:

"But ye are not in flesh, but in the Spirit, if so be that the Spirit of God dwells in you. Now if any man has not the Spirit of Christ, he is none of his". He is our comforter, our counselor, our advocate, and our teacher.

If you have not encountered the Holy Spirit in your life, Jesus promises to give you the Holy Spirit to be your counselor.

He says, ``If you love me, you will obey me and I will ask the Father and he will give you another counselor to be with you forever - the Spirit of Truth." (John 14:15 - 17).

So how can you receive the Holy Spirit?

Well, you must receive Jesus Christ as your personal savior first. All who are convicted of their sins, repent of their sins, confess their sins and accept Jesus as their personal savior will receive the Holy Spirit. <u>John 1:10-12</u> says He was in the World, and though the World did not recognize him. He came to that which was his own, but his own did not receive Him.

Yet to all who received him, to those who believed in his name, he gave the right to become Children of God".

Anyone who experiences salvation in Jesus Christ is given the Holy Spirit through the Baptism of the Holy Spirit.

John the Baptist says "I baptize you with water those who repent of their sins and turn to God. But someone is coming soon who is greater than I am - so much that I am not worthy even to be his slave and carry his sandals. He will baptize you with the Holy Spirit and fire" (Matthew 3:11). And that someone is Jesus Christ.

If Jesus baptizes with the Holy Spirit and fire, the question is: <u>Have you received the Holy Spirit since you became a</u> <u>Christian?</u>

Why do I need the Holy Spirit you may ask? You need the Holy Spirit because Jesus says "But the Counselor, the Holy Spirit, whom the Father will send in my name, <u>will teach you</u> all things and <u>will remind you</u> everything I have said to you (John 14:26). The Holy Spirit <u>will convict</u> the world of sin. "When He comes, he will convict the world of guilt in regard to sin and righteousness and judgment. In regard to sin because men do not believe in me; in regard to righteousness because I am going to the Father; and in regard to judg-

ment because the prince of this world now stands condemned" (John 16:8-11)

The Holy Spirit will be God's presence in the lives of believers.

"Do you not know that you yourselves are God's temple and that God's Spirit lives in you? If anyone destroys God's temple, God will destroy him, for God's temple is sacred, and you are that temple" (1 Corinthians 3: 16-17).

The Holy Spirit is the source of revelation, wisdom and power (1 Cor. 2:10-11) He guides us to all truth (John 16:13). He gives us spiritual gifts (1 Cor. 12:7-11) The Holy Spirit is a seal in the lives of believers (Ephesians 1:13).

He helps us in our weakness and intercedes for us (Romans 8:26-27). Lastly, the Holy Spirit sanctifies and enables us to bear good fruit in our lives. (Gal 5:16-26).

If you call yourself a Christian and have not received the Baptism of the Holy Spirit in your life, you are missing a great blessing in your life.

Jesus wants you to receive the Holy Spirit. The Holy Spirit will give you power to love Jesus as He loves you and you will serve Him unconditionally all the days of your life.

May God grant you the Spirit of Truth, the Comforter, the Advocate, the Spirit of God, the Oil of Gladness, the Spirit of Wisdom, the Spirit of Glory now and forevermore in the name of the Father, Son and the Holy Spirit. Amen.

---- CHAPTER 12 ----

TEXT: JOHN 10:1-10

TOPIC: "KNOWING THE GOOD SHEPHERD"

Greetings in the name of our Lord and Savior Jesus Christ.

This morning we want to look at verse 10 of John Chapter 10 where Jesus says: "The thief comes only to steal and kill and destroy; I have come that they may have life, and have it more abundantly."

This lesson on the Good Shepherd, is given in the context of John Chapter 9 where Jesus came across this blindman who had been blind from birth and Jesus made clay, put it in his eyes and told him to go to the pool of Siloam to wash it out. And when he washed, he was able to see.

It so happened that this took place on the Sabbath Day and Jesus violated two of the traditional observances of the Sabbath Day. According to their interpretation of the Sabbath Day law, it was unlawful to make clay on sabbath day. The fact that Jesus spit on the ground and made some mud with the saliva, and put it on the man's eyes, he violated their laws.

Secondly, it was unlawful to their interpretation to heal a man on the Sabbath Day. The fact that this miracle of healing, a man was able to see, because it happened on the Sabbath Day, riles the religious leaders.

They were angry. They first of all said well, he was not blind. It was just a story.

They examined his parents and found out that yes he was born blind. So they began to question him about how it happened. Tell us again.

And the man began to chide them sort of "Look, all I know is that I was blind and now I can see."

And you say that this man is a sinner but I don't know about that. I know that God does not hear the prayer of sinners. God obviously heard his prayer.

And they began to get angry with him. And they threw him out of the temple. They would not allow him to come again into the temple to worship God. He was excommunicated because of his declaration that he believed Jesus was a prophet. And so Jesus found the man and Jesus encouraged him.

And now in that context as he was talking to the man and said: "I come to open the eyes of the blind", the Pharisees were still there. So Jesus began to talk to them in the context of this man being excommunicated by the religious leaders from fellowship and worship in the temple. He said to them: "Truly, truly, I say to you, he who does not enter the sheepfold by the door but climbs in by another way, that man is a thief and a robber. (John 10:1-2). Referring to the religious leaders, those who had organized the religious system and those who had twisted it in order they might profit from it, He said they are thieves and robbers. You remember when he came to the temple and found them selling merchandise within the temple precinct, selling sacrifices and exchanging money, his statement was "You have made my Father's house a den of thieves" (Matthew 21:13).

So now again, he is calling them thieves "Those who have come after me. Those religious leaders who had sort to come in some other way, sort to come to God by something other than God's prescribed way, they are thieves. They are robbers.

One of the curses through the years are those who look upon religion as a way to control people and take advantage of them for their own personal financial gain.

Before Jesus came, there were many men who came claiming to be the Messiah. In the Book of Acts 4:34, Gameliel reminds the Pharisees concerning Theudas and concerning Judas of Galilee, many had come claiming to be the Messiah, who had gathered disciples around themselves. But those men who came claiming to be the Messiah, used the people to support their luxurious lifestyle that they were desiring. They lived in opulent-luxury, taking advantage of their followers.

It was the same during Jesus' time. Nothing had changed. The religious leaders were rude, arrogant, oppressive and wicked. They did not rejoice that this poor man has been healed.

Rather, they wanted to charge Jesus for violating the Sabbath rules. They showed contempt for the people they should have been tenderly shepherding. Instead of teaching the people, they ridiculed them for their ignorance. They used their power to keep the people in fear, threatening them with excommunication if they confessed Jesus to be the Christ (John 9:22).

Therefore, Jesus was showing us that the Pharisees were not faithful shepherds over the Lord's flock. He draws a sharp contrast between them as false shepherds whom He calls thieves and robbers (John 10: 1) and Himself as the True Shepherd, the Good Shepherd.

In the Old Testament, we have passages that picture the Lord as the Shepherd. In Psalm 23, we read "the Lord is my shepherd, I shall not want" (Psalm 23: 1).

In Ezekiel Chapter 34, God castigates then religious leaders of Israel for being self-centered, greedy shepherds who use the flock for their comfort and gain, but failed to care tenderly for the hurting. God pronounced judgment on those false shepherds and promised in Chapter 34:23

"Then I will set over them one shepherd, my servant David, and he will feed them; he will feed them himself and be their shepherd".

That prophecy was fulfilled by the Son of David, the Lord Jesus Christ, who is the Good Shepherd of His sheep (John 10:11).

So the story in John 10:1-10, gives us a symbolic picture of what happened in John Chapter 9, the healing of the blind man. It affirms the blindness of the Pharisees, the religious leaders who did not understand this picture. In our sermon passage, Jesus the true shepherd, is both rebuking the Pharisees who were listening to Him and warning his Followers, including the former blind man, not to follow these false shepherds who Jesus calls <u>thieves</u> and <u>robbers</u>.

Furthermore, He warns us in Matthew 7:15 to "Beware of the false prophets who come to you in sheep's clothing, but inwardly are ravenous wolves."

The <u>metaphor pictures</u> the deceptiveness and self-centered destructiveness of false prophets. They fool the sheep into thinking that they are sheep, and thus gain access to the flock. But their aim is not to build up and care for the flock, but to ravage them for their own selfish purposes.

Unfortunately, we still have false prophets and religious leaders today who deceive the flock, exploit them, abuse them, take advantage of them and fleece them of their hard-earned income. They never build or care for people. They seek to destroy. And unfortunately many churches have fallen into their traps and seen the result of their destruction. But thank God, we have the Good Shepherd, Jesus Christ the Lord who loves us and cares for us.

So what lesson do we learn from Christ's warning to us about false shepherds and false prophets?

We learn that in today's Christianity, we have many who profess to be Christians who neither enter through the "Gate" Jesus Christ into the Kingdom of God, nor obey His voice as the Good Shepherd.

We make the mistake of believing that we can enter the Kingdom of God by not going through the gate but by climbing over the wall. Those who seek salvation by climbing the wall or by any other means or ways, are thieves and robbers.

Are you a thief? Are you a robber? Are you seeking to enter the Kingdom of God through your good works, through your knowledge of the Bible, your education, your riches, your position, your power, and your influence? If you are, Jesus says you are a thief, and a robber. There is a slight difference between a thief and a robber.

Thieves tend to use cunning and deception to break into our house when we are gone from home or asleep and steal without us knowing.

Robbers on the other hand are more aggressive. They hold us at gunpoint and force us to give up our valuables. In both cases, they do not care about us. They only want to profit at our expense and use us to further their own selfish ends.

The Good Shepherd (Jesus) is warning us against such wicked and violent shepherds or Church leaders.

The question then is how can we protect ourselves from false prophets, false pastors, false church leaders?

The Good Shepherd gives us the answer. He says "My Sheep, hear my voice, and I know them, and they follow me" (John 10:27) Do you hear His voice? Do you follow Him?

Sadly, there are many of us who fail to hear His voice. We hear other voices that are not of the Good Shepherd.

We hear the voices of people who are godless, wicked, dangerous, evil, unrighteous, perverts, enticing and destructive. We follow them and unfortunately, suffer our destruction.

Jesus wants us to develop a close relationship with Him so that He can protect us and shepherd us to green pastures. To achieve this, <u>we must surrender</u> our life to Him. He invites us "<u>Come to me, all you who are weary and burdened, and I will</u> give you rest". <u>Take my yoke upon you and learn from me</u>, for I am gentle and humble in heart, and you will find rest for your souls" (Matthew 11:28-29)

1. <u>We must walk</u> with Him. David said "Yea though I walk through the valley of the shadow of death, I will fear no evil. For thou art with me, thy rod and thy staff they comfort me" (Psalm 23:4)
2. <u>We must seek His counsel</u> "And He will be called a Wonderful Counselor, Mighty God, Everlasting Father, Prince of Peace. (Isaiah 9:6).
3. <u>We must allow Him to lead us</u>: "He leaded me in the paths of righteousness for His name sake" (Psalm 23:3)
4. <u>Lastly, we must hear His voice</u>: "My sheep hear my voice, and I know them, and they follow me" (John 10:27). If we fail to hear His voice, we will fall victims to Satan's traps and manipulation. There is this store manager in Atlanta where I lived for 23 years before relocating to Arlington, Texas to pastor. He was robbed. But he was warned in time. Moments before the robbery, he was contacted by phone. "Are you the manager? Listen carefully; don't panic. This is the police. You are going to be robbed. DO NOT RESIST. Let the robber have your money. We will be waiting right outside your store and we need to catch him with the money on him. Thank you for your cooperation".

Moments later, sure enough, a man with a scruffy beard and a knife came demanding money. The manager took all of his cash out of the drawer and gave it to him. He watched the robber leave the store, waiting for the cops to close in.

Instead, the robber just got in his car and drove away. And as he saw the taillight disappear in the distance, he realized what had happened.

He realized that the call had not come from the police headquarters after all.

But from the thief. He listened to the wrong voice.

Jesus is right. "The thief comes only to steal and kill and destroy" (John 10:10). Do not listen to the voice of deception in your life. Listen to the voice of the Good Shepherd and follow Him.

The Good Shepherd gives eternal life, and gives it abundantly.

There are many conflicting, competing and deceptive voices out there trying to deceive us and rob us of the eternal promises of God. Learn to obey the voice of the Good Shepherd

- Jesus Christ the Lord.

Jesus is always whispering His love for us, He is calling us and wooing us into an ongoing relationship.

His voice goes before us, He guides and tells us who we are. If our hearts, souls and ears are tuned to Jesus' voice, we will hear His voice, Obey Him and follow Him.

He says "I am the Way, the Truth, and the Life; No one cometh into the Father but by me" (John 14:6).

Turn to Him, He is the Resurrected Savior, the Good Shepherd, the Bread of Life, the Light of the World, the Door of Salvation, the Resurrection and the Life, the Vine and the Alpha and Omega.

Come to Him for "Neither is there salvation in any other: for there is none other name under heaven given among men, whereby we must be saved" Jesus is the Savior, the Messiah, the Good Shepherd. (Acts 4:12)

May you hear His voice. May you obey Him.

May you follow Him.

In the name of the Father, Son and Holy Spirit. Amen.

CHAPTER 13

TEXT: JOHN 20:24-30

TOPIC: "OVERCOMING DOUBTS IN OUR LIVES"

Introduction:

Greetings in the precious name of the Lord Jesus. Last week, we learned about how to break the chains of fear in our lives.

Today, we want to look at how to overcome doubts in our lives.

Doubt is one of the major factors that impacts all of us. We doubt many things: our situations, relationship, friends, family, job, career, persons and about what the future holds for us.

The question is how can we access the power of the resurrection of Jesus to overcome our doubts?

In biblical theology, doubt is explained as the possibility to have questions, or doubt about persons, propositions or objects. Philosophically, doubt has been deemed a valuable element in honest rational inquiry.

Doubt prevents us from reaching hasty conclusions or making commitments to unreliable and untrustworthy sources. In the light of this definition, doubt is NOT an enemy of faith. This is seen clearly in Acts 17:11 in the attitude of the Berans who after hearing Paul preached, were motivated to search further and deeper in an understanding of faith.

However, in Biblical perspective, doubt carries a negative connotation. Our understanding of the Book of Isaiah Chapter 14 is that doubt actually began in heaven in the heart of Lucifer (Satan). Here, the object of doubt and rejection was the sovereignty and majesty of God (Isaiah 14:13-14).

On earth, doubt was conceived and given birth in the garden of Eden when the Serpent cast doubt on God's character and goodness (Genesis 3:1-5).

Tragically, Eve and Adam bought into the Serpent's deceptive plan and plunged humankind in the fall (Gen 3:6-19).

In both instances, doubt is clearly an aspect of sin. It is directed toward God and is characterized by rebellion and disobedience.

In the Gospels, the word "doubt" consistently carries with it a negative aspect, and the object of doubt again is always the Lord in some sense.

Peter doubted Christ's ability to keep him from drowning (Matthew 14:31). Here, doubt is small or weak faith. Peter became doubtful as to the Lord's reliability and power to sustain him

The Pharisees doubted Christ's messiahship and asked for another sign (Matt 12:38-42).

In Mark 11:23, we are told that if we have faith in God and do not "Doubt", we can move mountains and receive our request through prayer. Here, doubt is the opposite of faith.

Jesus encourages us in John 14:1 to not have a doubting heart with regards to the future, but believe in him, to trust him for our needs.

James 1:6-8 reminds us that a doubting man is an unstable or divided man who lacks sufficient faith to lay hold of the promises of God.

When we doubt in our heart, we sin against the Lord because we question the character, goodness and faithfulness of God. Here lies the importance of overcoming doubts in our lives as Christians.

A Christian Professor of Theology named Leon McKenzie writes that "we come into this world with question marks in our heads which never is fully erased".

We are not alone in our doubts.

Thomas in our Gospel lesson, doubted Jesus' resurrection.

Noah in the Old Testament doubted he could build a boat the size God wanted.

Moses doubted he could take on Pharaoh in Egypt and free his people.

Gideon doubted God's call on his life and tested God not once but twice.

Sarah doubted she could have children in her old age. And the list goes on and on.

Notice that all these Biblical characters doubted in their lives but overcame their doubts through faith to achieve great things for God.

The Gospel we have read today, says "Thomas (who was also called Twin) one of the Twelve, was not with the disciples when Jesus came. So the other disciples said to him: "We have seen the Lord". But he said to them, "Unless I see the nail marks in his hand and put my hand into his side, I will not believe it" (John 20:24-25).

This is a clear example of doubt and unbelief on the part of Thomas. But before we are quick to condemn Thomas, we must condemn ourselves too for we too, often doubt the Word and promises of God for us. We do not believe if we do not see a miracle and even after seeing miracles, we still scoff at them.

So how can we overcome our doubts? Well everything that took place on the resurrection morning, shows that Jesus' followers did not expect him to be resurrected from the dead.

<u>Doubt</u> and <u>fear</u> gripped them.

The women were afraid and trembling.

Mary Magdalene believes somebody has removed Jesus's body. Peter went to the empty tomb and wondered what happened?

Mary the Mother of James asked the gardener if he knew where they had taken Jesus' body to.

The disciples did not believe Mary's report.

When Jesus appeared, the disciples were afraid and thought He was a ghost and Thomas did not believe the other disciple's report.

So we clearly see that circumstances surrounding the disciples overwhelmed them and caused them to doubt the resurrection of Jesus. We too, like the disciples, are daily confronted by circumstances around us such as sickness, diseases, violence, unemployment, marital issues, job situations, and personal relationships, that cause us to doubt what the future holds for us and whether God's promises are true. Therefore, if we are to overcome doubts, we need to have faith in God and not look at our circumstances. Jesus says "Blessed are those that believe without seeing me". Let us obey His Word for doubt is caused by Satan (Genese 3:4), by unbelief (Luke 1:18-20), by worldly wisdom (1 Corinthians 1:18-25) and by spiritual instability (James 1:6-7).

When we entertain doubts, we also entertain fear in our lives. Doubt and fear cause us to become immobilized, paralyzed, unproductive, unfruitful and crippled in our lives.

Right now, there are many of us in the same situation because God wants us to overcome our doubts and fears. He encourages you in Deuteronomy 31:6 to "Be strong and courageous. Do not be afraid or terrified because of them, for the Lord your God goes with you; he will never leave you not forsake you".

Secondly, if we are to overcome our doubts we must avoid doubt-pushers.

Doubt-pushers are people who have the ability to discourage themselves as well as others around them.

We see in Numbers 13:25-33 that when a dozen spies went over Israel, the very land that God had prepared to give them, to scout for invasion, ten came back and said they were not able to defeat the people while two said yes they could.

Now these ten doubters experienced the same things the other two spies did.

They went to the same place, spent the same amount of time and had the same experience and yet, they came away with radically different conclusions.

Doubters always turn the conversation from positive to negative.

They have the capability that no matter how good something is, they always find the negative. Do you know anybody like that? Oh yes. I know one that I will never forget.

Years ago, while serving as pastor in West Africa, I went to visit a sick member at the hospital. While praying and encouraging the sick person, some members of the Church also came to visit the same sick member. Everything was going well until a doubt-pusher among them decided to run his mouth. When this doubt pusher learned of the kind of illness, instead of comforting the sick, he started saying "this sickness is dangerous. It kills people just like that". And he said it without shame, or compassion. You could imagine my anger. Here I was trying to minister to a sick person only for this guy to destroy the faith of the sick person with discouraging words.

Doubt-pushers are a very bad influence on our faith, life and trust in God. Avoid them.

Lastly, we must all try to overcome our doubts by learning from the experience of Thomas the Apostle. People will judge us by one sad mistake in our life. Thomas' words "Except I see in his hands the print of the nail, and thrust my hand into his side, I will not believe" (John 20:25), will always follow him.

The epithet "Doubting Thomas" has unfortunately become a blot on his life. And he is not alone.

When we think of David, we think of his sin. We forget what a great man he was in spite of his failure.

When we think of Jacob, we think of how he stole his brother's birthright.

When we think of Peter, we remember his denial of Jesus three times

William Shakespeare, an English poet, playwright and actor said: The evil that men do lives after them. The good is often interred with their bones". This is what happened to Thomas the Apostle. No doubt he showed great faith many times, but we remember him because of his doubt about the resurrection.

Yet in reality, he was one of the most steadfast and loyal apostles among the Twelve.

Conclusion:

I know we all have our doubts. We have doubts whether we will be healed of our diseases, whether our marriages will last the test of time, whether our Children or grandchildren will succeed in life. We doubt our job situations, our career, education, business and relationships. Whatever our doubts are, let us not make the mistake of riding on the wings of doubt in our lives.

Doubt will cripple us, diminish our faith in God and in his promises for us.

It is true that we are living in challenging times: times of uncertainty, times of pandemics, times of economic and political troubles. But we need to rise above in God who has promised to take care of us no matter what challenges we go through in life.

In Jeremiah 29:11 our God declares "For I know the plans I have for you, plans to prosper you and not to harm you, plans to give you hope and a future".

His promises are sure, true and irrevocable. I encourage you to stay faithful to God. Do not doubt Him. Keep trusting Him, keep following Him, keep serving Him and keep praying.

He will show you the nail prints and you will, like Thomas, affirm that indeed, He is "My Lord and my God".

May God Almighty the Father, Son and the Holy Spirit dispel your doubts and fears about every <u>unpredictable</u>, unimaginable, unbelievable, unfavorable, and unpleasant circumstances in your life.

May He bless you with wisdom, power, courage, faith and cover you in His righteousness now and forever more in the name of the Father, Son and the Holy Spirit. Amen.

Chapter 14

TEXT: MATTHEW 21:1-11 (MARK 11:1-10)

TOPIC: "HOSANNA" OR "CRUCIFY HIM" WHICH SIDE ARE YOU?

Introduction:

Today is Palm Sunday. It is a day that commemorates the entrance of Jesus into Jerusalem when Palm branches were placed in his path, before his arrest on Holy Thursday and his crucifixion on Good Friday. Palm Sunday marks the beginning of Holy Week - the final week of Lent.

On that Palm Sunday, the sun was rising rapidly, it was beginning to shoot its golden arrows across the horizon to <u>gild</u> the sky and curtain off the dawn that would bring a new day to the history filled city of Jerusalem.

This was the festive season of Passover. The old city was filled with pilgrims, visitors, and travelers who had come from many countries to share in the feast. Secular census records indicate there were at least 2.5 million people in Jerusalem for the event.

An exciting rumor spread through the city that Jesus Christ is coming.

Behind Jesus were His sermons, ahead, His suffering. Behind Him were His parables, ahead, His passion.

Behind Him were His suppers of fellowship; ahead His last Supper of betrayal.

Behind Him the delights of Galilee; ahead, dark Gethsemane. Prophecy was now to become practice.

Jesus had spent the night at the home of friends in Bethany on the opposite side of the Mount of Olives from Jerusalem. The two towns were no more than five miles apart. Historians tell us that traditionally persons from various regions all had their special area around Jerusalem where they camped for feast days.

The south end of the Mount of Olives had for many years been the camping grounds of people from Galilee.

These were the unsophisticated and unspoiled people of the area where Jesus spent most of His time and performed most of His miracles. They knew Him best.

On several occasions, the Bible says they had tried to make Jesus a king (John 6:15).

Mark 12:37 says of them, "The Common people heard Him gladly"

The Galileans were the common people with whom He was popular.

But there was another group of people

In the city of Jerusalem, were the wealthy and superficially religious leaders.

Jesus had antagonized them be referring to the Scribes and Pharisees as hypocrites (Matthew 23).

Also among them were the Sadducees who had long been plotting to kill Jesus.

In order to preserve their wealth and lifestyle, they had consorted with the conquering Romans. In doing so, they compromised their faith.

They had much to lose if they displeased their Roman overlords.

These man-pleasing priests and scribes plotted their nefarious death scheme.

The poorer Galileans had nothing to lose. But the city dwellers would do anything to <u>satisfy</u> the Romans in order to continue to prosper.

To them the issue was "<u>show me the money.</u>" In their eyes, Jesus was <u>expendable</u>. Besides, in the eyes of the religious leaders, He was a threat to religious tradition. They did not believe Jesus is the Messiah. In the Book of Mark 11:9, we see two groups. "<u>Those who went before</u>" and "<u>those who followed</u>".

Those that went before Him, were persons who had come out of Jerusalem because of their curiosity as a result of all the shouting.

Those who followed and cried out were Galileans.

If we read the text distant from the event, it may cause us to merge the two crowds into one and assume it was the same people who shouted "Hosanna" that also cried "Crucify Him".

But the truth is that it was the <u>jubilant</u> Galileans who shouted "Hosanna" and the <u>aristocratic, superficially religious ingrates of Jerusalem who wanted to appease the Romans who cried</u> "<u>Crucify Him</u>".

As we celebrate Palm Sunday today, I wonder which crowd our actions would relate to. Are we the jubilant Galileans shouting "Hosanna" or the aristocratic, superficially religious ingrates of Jerusalem shouting "Crucify Him"? Unfortunately, many of we are like the superficially religious ingrates of Jerusalem. We daily put Jesus to open shame in our speech, actions or lifestyle - and that means we shout "Crucify Him"

The event of Palm Sunday. The timing of Jesus' triumphant entry into Jerusalem is amazing and at the right-time. It was in fulfilment of prophecy. This was the week of preparation for the celebration of the passover feast.

It was a celebration commemorating the deliverance of Jesus from Egyptian captivity. It always occurred on the 15th of the Jewish month of Nisan. That is about mid-April for us. All who lived within 20 miles of Jerusalem were required to attend. Actually, Jews from all over the world gladly gathered for this major happening.

As excitement mounts with the approach of our holidays, an air of Joy preceded it.

Roads were repaired, tombs were whitewashed and children were rehearsed in the significance of the event.

The Prophet Daniel foretold when this momentous event would occur in Daniel 9:24-26. I quote "Seventy weeks of years are decreed concerning your people and your holy city, to finish the transgression, to put an end to Sin, and to atone for iniquity, to bring in everlasting righteousness, to seal both vision and prophet, and to anoint a most holy place".

Jesus went to Bethany six days before passover (John 12:1) and entered Jerusalem the next day, April 6, 32. That was precisely 490 years from the time of Daniel's prophecy.

By this act, God the Father was not only validating Jesus as the Messiah, to the world, but also dramatizing for us the fact that He keeps His word through prophecy, throughout the Old Testament. Here are prophecies about the coming Messiah.

Prophetically it was written Messiah would be a descendant of Abraham (Genesis 12:3), Isaac (Genesis 17:19), and Jacob (Numbers 24:17). It was written He would be from the Tribe of Judah (Genesis 49:10) and heir to the throne of David (Isaiah 9:7).

So God the Father wanted God the Son to be well identified on His visit to earth. Jesus' triumphant entry into Jerusalem at the appointed time, fulfilled every prophecy about the Messiah.

Furthermore the prophet Zechariah (Zechariah 9:9) said the Messiah would enter Jerusalem riding on a donkey. All those along the route He was to ride, had learned in infancy and repeated often the prophet.

"Rejoice greatly, O daughter of Zion shout, daughter of Jerusalem! Behold, your King is coming to you; He is just and having salvation, lowly and riding a donkey. A colt, the foal of a donkey" (Zechariah 9:9)

So the triumphant entry of Jesus in Jerusalem was not something that just happened accidentally. It was in fulfillment of prophecy. God the Father had planned our salvation even before the foundation of the earth was laid. And through prophecies in the Torah (the five books of Moses), and the Prophets has revealed to us who the Messiah will be Jesus. There are many who still do not believe or affirm Jesus as the Messiah. But this even of Palm Sunday in the year April 6, 32 is God's affirmation to us that Jesus is the Messiah who came to gives us new life.

Therefore, as we celebrate this Palm Sunday let us meditate on three lessons

1. He came to cleanse.

Christ came to the temple to cleanse it spiritually from hypocritical defilement and that is what He wants to do in our lives. Our lives are full of sin and unrighteousness, full hypocritical defilement and wickedness. Jesus came to cleanse us from our sins and to make us new creatures.

1 Corinthians 5:17 says "Therefore if any person be in Christ, he or she is a new creature: old things have passed away; behold, all things have become new". This Palm Sunday, let us not sing

"Hosanna" Hosanna, Hosanna and fail to give our lives to Jesus the Messiah for total spiritual transformation.

2. <u>He came to forgive.</u>

Jesus is called "King and Lord". Is He the one you respect who has authority over you as your divine God? Throughout the Bible, God has shown us His forgiving love: (Numbers 14:18). The Lord is slow to anger and abound in steadfast love, forgiving iniquity and transgression, but he will by no means clear the guilty" (Number 14:18).

<u>Numbers 15:28</u>

"And a priest shall make atonement before the Lord for the person who makes a mistake, when they sin unintentionally, to make atonement for him, and he shall be forgiven.

<u>I John 1:9</u>

"If we confess our sins, he is faithful and just to forgive us our sins and to cleanse us from all unrighteousness"

<u>Psalm 86:5</u>

"For you, o Lord, are good and forgiving, abounding in steadfast love to all who call upon you"

God the Father, sent God the Son Jesus to come and save us from our sins and He is waiting for us to ask for His help, and He will be there with love and forgiveness.

3. <u>He came to identify with His followers.</u>

In that crowd of common people on the Mount of Olives who shouted "Hosanna" meaning "Let even the angels in the highest heights of heaven cry unto God, save now!" were persons who owed Jesus gratitude for their restored sight, for straight limbs, for clear same reasoning, and healed bodies; even one named Lazarus, his life restored from the grave.

We, like them, must be indebted to Jesus as we celebrate this Palm Sunday. Let our shouts of "Hosanna" be truly from our hearts.

Chapter 15

TEXT: GENESIS 22: 1-14

TOPIC: "WHEN YOUR FAITH IS TESTED"

Introduction: Greetings in the name of our Lord and Saviour Jesus Christ. Our topic for meditation today is "When your Faith is Tested" or "Faith Fully Surrendered"

Trials and tribulations are one of the few certainties we have in life. None of us can escape the peaks and valleys we encounter, and it is easy to feel inadequate when sharing our trials.

James 1:24 says, "Count it all joy, my brothers, when you meet trials of various kinds, for you know that the testing of your faith produces steadfastness. And let steadfastness have its full effect, that you may be perfect and complete, lacking nothing"

Today, we shall look at the life of Abraham and how his faith in God was tested and the lessons we can learn to help us stand the test of trials in our lives. The story we have just read from Genesis 22:1-14, speaks of Abraham the Patriarch.

He was born around 2166 BC. Nothing is known of his early life or how he was led to God. Yet the importance of his life cannot be underestimated. He is mentioned some 308 times in the Bible, 234 times in the Old Testament and 11 times in the New Testament.

Abraham was born and raised in Ur of Chaldees, a city located in the land of Mesopotamia. Ur was the seaport on the Persian Gulf, at the mouth of the Euphrates River. Prior to his conversion, Abraham was a worshipper of idols.

Then God appeared to him and Abraham became a believer.

In Chapter 12 of the Book of Genesis, we read about the call of Abraham, He was commanded by God to leave Mesopotamia for a new land that God had promised to show him.

At the age of 75 and his wife Sarah was 65, Abraham received from God the sevenfold features of what we call the Abrahamic Covenant.

1. I will make of thee a great nation
2. I will bless thee
3. I will make thy name great.
4. Thou shalt be a blessing.
5. I will bless them that bless thee.
6. I will curse him that curseth thee.
7. In thee shall families of the earth be blessed

4. Twenty five years after this covenant, in Chapter 17 of Genesis, we read that when Abraham was 99 years old, God gave Abraham the sign of the covenant. "You shall be the ancestor of a multitude of nations" (Gen 17:4). "But the Covenant I will establish with Isaac whom Sarah shall bear to you at this season next year". (Gen 17:21). The sign of covenant was circumcision of the flesh of his foreskin. Abraham circumcised at the age of 99 together with every male in his family.

In Chapter 18:10 of the Book of Genesis, we read that a son is promised to Abraham and Sarah: "I will surely return to you in due season and your wife Sarah shall have a son". In chapter 21, we learn about the birth of Isaac to Abraham and Sarah.

Abraham was 100 years old and Sarah was 90 years old.

The occasion was a great joy to both parents. Isaac was weaned and later a great feast was held to celebrate the occasion.

It was after this that our text for today came in. Our text says: "After these things": God commanded Abraham to offer up as a burnt offering or sacrifice his son Isaac on Mount (Moraya). At this time, Abraham was living at Beer-sheba and he had to walk 50 miles for three days with Isaac and his two servants to the land of Moriah to offer Isaac as a sacrifice to the Lord.

Put yourself in Abraham's shoes. You are 100 years old. Your wife is 90 years old. You have never had a child in your life except in your old age when God blessed you with a male child Isaac. You and your wife are very happy that at last you now have a male child who will carry on the family tree from generation to generation.

And now God appears to you and commands you to sacrifice your only son to Him. How will you feel? Will you tell your wife?

Will you agree to obey God's command? I bet many of us will refuse. We will say God is not fair. We will find excuses to disobey God. And some of us will surely lose our faith and trust in God.

But not Abraham. Abraham had faith in God.

- Abraham feared or reverence God
- Abraham worshipped God sincerely and
- Abraham was committed to God.

If you follow the story, you find that Abraham indeed arrived at Mount Moriah to sacrifice Isaac as commanded by God. Even when Isaac asked his father: "My father, behold the fire and the wood; but where is the lamb for a burnt offering? Abraham with faith in God, responded: "God will provide himself the lamb for a burnt offering, my son" What a faith!!! Think about Abraham tying his son Isaac up and putting him on the bundles of wood to sacrifice Isaac for God. Think about him drawing his knife, raising it up and preparing to stab Isaac to death. And think about God's intervention: God calls Abraham and says to him: "Do not lay your hand on the lad or do anything to him; for now I know that you fear God, seeing you have not withheld your son, your only son, from me. And think about the ram that was caught in a thicket by his horns which Abraham took and offered it up as a burnt offering instead of his son. This is a moving story with a good ending but the lessons learnt are incredible.

5. This morning, I want to tie the lessons we learn from Abraham's experience with God to our own lives and our relationship with God. As Christians, like Abraham, God is commanding us to sacrifice certain things in our lives on Mount Moraya - our altar - for him.

1. The first is our lives.

The Bible says: "There is a way that appears to be right, but in the end it leads to death. We can see how this event in the life of Abraham was a shadow of things to come, where God tells us to trust Him, then provides for us. It began all the way back to the beginning in the Garden of Eden. Sin caused a separation between God and mankind. Sin caused the first death; the animals which had their skin used to cover Adam and Eve.

And God required a blood sacrifice to atone for sin.

When God told Abraham to take his only son Isaac, to a place to sacrifice him, God was foreshadowing that He would sacrifice His only begotten Son Jesus to die on Calvary for our sins.

When Abraham told Isaac that God would provide the sacrifice, God did through a ram. In the same way God has provided His own sacrifice for our sins through Jesus.

The question is: Have you trusted God for the sacrifice He made for you?

Have you trusted Jesus as your Lord and Savior or you are trying to supply your own sacrifice?

The best sacrifice we can bring to God in worship is <u>our lives</u>, <u>our bodies</u>, <u>our time</u>, <u>our service</u>, and <u>our tithes</u>.

The Apostle Paul entreats us to therefore by the mercies of God, to present our bodies as a living sacrifice, holy and acceptable to God which is your spiritual worship. (Rom 12:1).

Have you laid it all on the altar of God?

2. The second command is about Tithes/Offering

Like Abraham, God is commanding us to sacrifice our <u>Isaac</u> which is our Tithes and offering on Mount Moriah, the altar of God.

In Leviticos 27:30 God says:

All tithes from the land, whether the seed from the ground or the fruit from the tree are the Lords; they are holy to the Lord".

In Exodus 23:19, we read: The choices of the first fruits of your ground you shall bring into the house of the Lord your God".

God expects us to make tithing as part of our Life in Christ. There are three reasons why God wants us to give our tithes and offerings

a) <u>Giving our tithes and offering expresses</u> our gratitude to God for the <u>gifts of life</u> and for the <u>blessings we have received</u> and continue to receive daily in our lives. When we give our tithes, we are grateful for what God has done and is doing for us. It is our "thank you to God".

b) <u>Giving our tithes and offering</u> is a way to renew our faith and grow closer to Christ.

c) <u>Giving our tithes and offering</u> is a way to help our church remain strong and to fulfil the mission of the Church which is "To make disciples of Jesus Christ for the transformation of the world".

When we give our tithes with loving generous hearts, God will reward us with joy and fulfillment. The Bible says "the measure you give will be the measure you get back" (Luke 6:38).

- Abraham had faith in God - Do you have faith in God?
- Abraham obeyed God's command - Do you obey God's command to tithe and give offerings?
- Abraham revered God - Do you respect God?
- Abraham worshipped God sincerely - Do you worship God in Tithes and offering?

Back to the story of Abraham. After the episode involving Abraham and Isaac, God testified about Abraham that "Now I know that you fear God, since you have not withheld your son, your only son from me" (Gen 22:12)

The question to us is: Can God testify about you that "Now I know that you fear God, since you have not withheld your tithes, offering, time, service and devotion from me"?

If God cannot testify this about you, then it is time for you to evaluate your relationship with God as a Christian and do what God commands you to do.

Abraham was richly blessed because he obeyed God. You can also be blessed if you stop giving excuses about giving your life, tithes, offerings to God through worship.

Worshipping God means we must give unto God the glory due His name. We must worship Him in the beauty of holiness (Psalm 29:2).

We are warned: There shall be no foreign god among you; nor shall you worship any other god" (Psalm 81:9).

And Jesus says: You shall worship the Lord your God, and Him only you shall serve" (Matt 4:10).

We cannot, therefore, worship God in our sins. God is holy. Jesus died to take away our sins to enable us to worship God in spirit and truth. It cost the Son of God his life to save us so we might worship God as we are doing now. In return, <u>what is your sacrifice to God for all he has done for you in life</u>? Will you continue to rob Him of <u>tithes and offerings</u>; <u>your time</u>, <u>your service</u>, <u>your life</u>, and <u>your devotion</u>? <u>Think about it</u>.

May the Lord God Almighty help us to become like Abraham who was prepared to sacrifice everything to God even his only Son Isaac in the name of the Father and of the Son and of the Holy Spirit. Amen.

Chapter 16

TEXT: MATTHEW 25:31-46

TOPIC: "JUDGEMENT DAY"

<u>Introduction:</u> Since June 7, this year, we have been preaching from the Book of Matthew from Chapter 9 through Chapter 25 following this year's lectionary. The book of Matthew is the first Gospel of the account of Jesus' life and ministry of the New Testament. Matthew presents Jesus as the Messiah (1:1), the promised descendant of King David who would bring God's Kingdom to earth and establish a time of peace and justice.

Right from Chapter 20 onwards, Jesus told his disciples that "The Son of man came to give his life as a ransom for many" He reminds them that "A man sent his son to his tenants, but they killed him" in chapter 21.

In chapter 22, Jesus said: "The Kingdom is like a wedding" and when the Pharisees questioned Him about the law, He said "Love God and your neighbor". Jesus reminds us in Chapter 23 that the Pharisees preach but do not practice what they preach.

Then from Chapters 24-25, we read about Jesus' last discourse in this Gospel.

In His last discourse before he went to the cross, Jesus denounces the Scribes and Pharisees, laments over Jerusalem, deals with eschatology - the end time.

Jesus also prophecies persecution (24: 9-14) and the desolating sacrilege (24:15-28), and tells the coming of the son of Man (24:29-31).

He gives the lesson of the fig tree (24:32-35) and tells of the necessity of watchfulness (24:36-44).

Jesus' discourse includes several parables that emphasize preparation for the master's (Jesus) return.

- The parable of the faithful and unfaithful servant (24:45-50), where readiness for Christ's coming consists of being found at work when the master arrives.
- The Parable of the Wise and Foolish virgins (25:1- 13), where readiness consists of carefully checking preparations before sleeping.
- The parable of the Talents (25:14-30), preached last sunday by Pastor Kate, where readiness consists of faithful stewardship over that which the master has provided.

Today, Jesus concludes His Eschatological Discourse with the Judgement of the Nations (25:31-46), which portrays Judgement Day. Readiness here consists of faithfulness in "the least of these" ministry.

In this final teaching, the Lord Challenges every disciple of Jesus Christ to be a messenger or witness of God's kingdom in a broken world.

The setting of this event is at the beginning of the millennium after the tribulation - the millennial kingdom is the title given to the 1,000 - reign of Jesus Christ on the earth when He returns a second time. All those on earth at that time will be brought before the Lord, and He will separate them "as a shepherd separates the sheep from the goats. He will put the sheep on his right and the goats on his left (verse 32-33). The sheep are those who were saved during the tribulation; the goats are the unsaved who survived the tribulation.

The sheep on Jesus' right hand are blessed by God the Father and given an inheritance. The reason is stated; "For I was hungry and you gave me something to eat, I was thirsty and you gave me something to drink, I was a stranger and you invited me in, I needed clothes and you clothed me, I was sick and you looked after me, I was in prison and you came to visit me (verses 35-36)

The righteous will not understand: when did they see Jesus in such a pitiful condition and help Him? "The King will reply, "I tell you the truth, whatever you did for one of the least of these brothers of mine, you did for me" (Verse 39-40).

The goats on Jesus' left hand are cursed with eternal hell-fire, "prepared for the devil and his angels (verse 41). The reason is given: they had the opportunity to minister to the Lord, but they did nothing (verses 42-43). The damned ask, "Lord, when did we see you hungry or thirsty or a stranger or needing clothes or sick or in prison, and did not help you?" (verse 44).

Jesus replies, I tell you the truth, whatever you did not do for one of the least of these, you did not do for me" (verse 45).

Jesus then ends the discourse with a contrast; "They will go away to eternal punishment, but the righteous to eternal life (verse 46).

In this parable of the sheep and goats, we are looking at man redeemed and saved, and man condemned and lost.

A casual reading seems to suggest that salvation is the result of good works. The "sheep" acted charitably, giving food, drink, and clothing to the needy. The "goats" showed no charity. This seems to result in salvation for the sheep and the damnation for the goats.

But far be from it, the scripture does not contradict itself, and the bible clearly and repeatedly teaches that salvation is by faith through the grace of God not by our good works (ref John 1:12, Acts 15:11, Romans 3:22-23, Romans 7:24-25, and Ephesians 2:8-10).

In fact Jesus Himself makes it clear in the parable that salvation of the "sheep" is not based on their works - their inheritance was theirs "since the creation of the world" (Matt 25:34), long before they could ever do any good works.

The good works mentioned in the parable are not the cause of salvation but the <u>effect</u> of salvation. As Christians we become like Christ as recorded in Romans 8:29, 2 Corinthians 3:18 and Colossians 2:6-7.

Galatians 5:22 tells us that the fruit of the Spirit is love, joy, peace, patience, kindness, goodness, gentleness, faithfulness, and self-control. Therefore good works in a Christians life are the direct overflow of these traits, and are only acceptable to God because of the relationship that exists between servant and master, the saved and their savior, the sheep and their shepherd (Ephesians 2:10).

So the core message of this parable of the sheep and goats is that God's people will love others. Good works will result from our relationship to the shepherd.

Followers of Christ will <u>treat others with kindness, serving them as if they were serving Christ Himself</u>.

The unsaved, the unregenerate live in the opposite manner. While "goats" can indeed perform acts of kindness and charity, <u>their hearts are not right with God, and their actions are</u> <u>not for the right purpose</u> - to honor and worship God.

So the main lesson for us is "we need to show love to those who seem least important"

This parable took place at the Mount of Olives, in a private conversation between Jesus and His disciples only days before His death (Matt 26:1-2).

Jesus portrays the righteous, who have gone beyond simply <u>mouthing their faith</u>, as unaware of the significance of the good they have done. Jesus identifies with the needy when He equates service done for them as being done for Him.

What a contrast to the self-righteous attitude of many Christians and religious leaders, who flaunted their religiously correct-activities, done primarily for their own benefit. They were unaware of the needs of the people around them. It was not that they were actively doing wrong, but that they were not doing what was right in helping the needy, thus ignoring much of the teaching in the scriptures.

As we end our series of sermons from the Book of Matthew, the conclusion is that

"The Son of Man (Jesus) will come in glory with angels; He will sit on His throne in heaven glory. All of the nations will be separated like shepherds separate sheep and goats. The sheep will be on Jesus' right, a place of honor and the goats will be on His left - a place of dishonor.

The question for us is: "Will we be a sheep or a goat"?

As individuals and as a church, this parable challenges us to begin to take ministry to the poor and needy seriously. From today onwards, do not turn your attention away from those in need in our Church, our community and on family. Their faces are the faces of Jesus.

May the Lord grant that when that Judgement day comes, we will be part of the sheep that will be on His right hand for the reward prepared for us since the foundation of the world in the name of the Father, Son and Holy Spirit. Amen.

— Chapter 17 —

TEXT: MATTHEW 13:24-37

TOPIC: "WHATEVER YOU DO, DO NOT FALL ASLEEP"

Introduction: Today is the last Sunday of the church year. During this last Sunday of the church year, the message in Mark 13:24-37 is a message that advises us as followers of Jesus Christ, to stay alert to stay awake, to not get too comfortable, or grow complacent. Whatever we do, Jesus reminds us not to fall asleep for the day is coming. It is coming soon and time is short. Jesus is coming again soon!

The text reminds us that the imminent return of Jesus is foundational to the Christian faith. His record promises to come back are too numerous to list. Which makes the loss of a sense of urgency, the lack of anticipation, and the absence of vigilance in the Church an indictment of Christians for failing to believe what we confess in the apostles' creed "From thence he will come to judge the quick and the death". Observers could be forgiven for questioning whether we mean it.

The last Sunday in the church year should not be the only time we talk about His return. But a sermon on this text misses the point if it does not call the hearer to a life of attentive and active vigilance. Vigilance, as a concept, is not foreign to any of us. We all know what it means to be on guard. Airport announcements continually remind fliers to look out for unattended baggage. Parents of small children watch alertly when anyone takes more than a passing interest in their little ones.

Parents of teenagers stay up late hoping and praying their young drivers will come home in one piece.

Credit card companies actively monitor purchases to catch fraud before it gets out of hand. Deer hunters notice every bouncing squirrel and every falling leaf from deer stands. College applicants develop 20/20 vision for any and every potential scholarship.

And Jesus used a fig tree and a master's journey to teach his first-century hearers, lessons on vigilance. Today, preachers use similar contemporary images to teach what it means to be vigilant. The point is that people of every age know what it means to be vigilant. So, our text today is teaching us to be vigilant about the second coming of the Lord Jesus Christ.

The context of this Bible lesson begins with verse 1 of Chapter 13 with a comment by one of the disciples about the temple: "Look, teacher, what large stones and what large building!". Jesus responds by predicting the destruction of the temple (verse 2).

The temple was the center of Jewish worship and life, but its days are numbered. The new center of worship and life will be the son of Man. Peter, James and John (Jesus' inner circle plus Andrew asked: "When will this be and what will be the sign that all these things are about to be accomplished?" Jesus responded with a lengthy discourse dealing with the question "when" and the "signs" question by telling of <u>false messiahs and false prophets,</u> <u>wars and rumours of war,</u> <u>earthquakes and famines,</u> <u>persecutions,</u> <u>betrayal by family members,</u> <u>the darkening of the sun and moon,</u> and <u>the falling of stars</u> (verses 7-25).

At the time of the writing of this Gospel of Mark, Christians were experiencing persecution. Jerusalem had been destroyed. This chapter presents Jesus' promise that time is moving toward the coming of the Son of Man, who will gather all the people together and make all things right. Unfortunately, the Church today is divided between Christians who expect expectantly the return of the Son of Man and Christians who ignore this aspect of Jesus' teaching altogether.

Nevertheless, we need to take Jesus' words in Mark 13 as seriously as we take Jesus' words elsewhere. The promise is that God has prepared something wonderful beyond our world and time. Shouldn't we be happy at the prospect of Christ coming to set our world right once again?

While this is encouraging, it is also demanding. Jesus places a high premium on faithful discipleship in the midst of terrible trials. He calls us to endure and to be watchful.

Spiritual alertness is as important as physical security. We live in a world full of soul killing temptations and distractions. We are regularly subjected to advertising that trivializes life.... to friends who. demand that we do bad things --- to movies that glamorize violence, drugs, and sex --- to a thousand tempters. The list of temptations is endless. When we succumb to them, we (and our family and friends) suffer consequences. "Watch, keep alert", Jesus warns "For you do not know when the time is. Paul warned that the day of the Lord would come like a thief in the night. Then people who had been emphasizing peace and safety will experience sudden destruction. He counsels, "So then let's not sleep, as the rest do, but let us watch and be sober" (1 Thessalonians 5:2-3, 6).

So during this last Sunday of the church year, our readings this month have dealt with the end times before Christ's return. That is what we find in Mark 13, Jesus' eschatological discourse, his teaching about the last things.

The question: is are we eagerly and expectantly looking for our Lord's return? Or are we instead sleepwalking our way through life? If so, then today Jesus is giving us a needed wake-up call. "Stay awake!" because the world all around us is sleeping spiritually. They are oblivious to the thought of Christ coming again. They may be very busy, hustling and bustling to and from, running around like a chicken with its head cut off.

Lots of shopping to do: Black Friday, Cyber Monday and Sundays as the Lord's Day gets lost in the shuffle. The people of this world may be busy, but spiritually they are asleep. They are not conscious or cognizant, not thinking at all about the end times and eternity, about one's relationship with God, and the fact that this world is indeed coming to an end, and after that, the judgment.

But Christ would not have his people be so sleepy and dullminded and stuck in a state of insensitivity. Jesus would have us be awake and alert and ready for his return. And until then, Christ would have us be active and doing the work he has given us to do, before the night comes, when no man can work. That is the point of this discourse to Jesus' disciples in Mark Chapter 13.

What about you? What about us? What are we waiting for?

Jesus tells us: "But in those days, after that tribulation, the sun will be darkened, and the moon will not give its light, and the stars will be falling from heaven, and the powers in the heavens will be shaken. And then they will see the Son of Man coming in clouds with great power and glory. And then he will send out his angels and gather his elect from the four winds, from the ends of the earth to the ends of heaven."

That is what we are waiting for. Jesus will come again in great glory. There will be cosmic disruption on a scale never seen before. The heavens will start shaking and falling apart. New heaven and a new earth are coming. Christ himself is coming, the mighty Messiah revealed in his full majesty. And he is coming for us, for his whole Church to be with him forever, sharing in his glory.

For the unbelievers, for the children of the world, it will be a day of terror and dread. For us though, it will be a great day of rejoicing and redemption.

Jesus could be coming back this afternoon. Or it could be a week from now. Or a year. Or a hundred years from now. No one knows. And because no one knows, the important thing is to be ready for his return at any time. The question is: Are you ready? If Jesus comes back this afternoon, are you ready?

And this raises the question: How does one become ready? How do we stay awake and keep awake, so that we are ready at all times?

The answer is found in these words of Jesus: "Heaven and earth will pass away, but my words will not pass away". (Matthew 24:35).

The world as we know it is not going to last. Do not put all your eggs in that basket.

This life with all its wealth and pleasures and possessions will pass away. We will pass away. And what we do, there will be what then? Nothing to hang unto.

However, there is something secure and lasting and eternal we can hold onto. It is the word of the Lord Jesus Christ. Jesus' words will certainly never pass away.

You can count on them.

You can stake your life, and your eternal life, on the words of Christ.

But while we wait for His second coming again, whatever we do, let us not fall asleep.

Let us occupy ourselves with worshipping and serving the Lord for -- He has commanded us to make disciples of all nations, to love God with all our heart, soul and mind, to love our neighbour as ourselves, to minister to the poor and needy, and to bless those who persecute or curse us for He has promised to be with us even unto the end of the world. Let us therefore <u>stay awake</u>, <u>be watchful</u>, prayerful, and alert every day of our lives and may the blessings of Almighty God the Father, the Son and the Holy Spirit be with us forever and ever Amen.

--- CHAPTER 18 ---

TEXT: MARK 1:1-8

TOPIC: "THE GOOD NEWS OF JESUS CHRIST"

Introduction: Today is the Second Sunday in Advent. For many Christians unfamiliar with the liturgical year, there may be some confusion surrounding the meaning of Advent. Some people may know that the Advent season focuses on expectation and think that it serves as an anticipation of Christ's birth in the season leading up to Christmas. This is part of the story, but there is more to Advent.

Advent is a time of <u>expectation and hope</u>. Advent means "<u>arrival</u>" or "<u>coming</u>", and it prompts us to pause each day in December and remember why Jesus came at Christmas. Traditions vary by country, but common ways of commemorating Jesus' birth are through <u>Advent calendars, wreaths, and candles</u>. Advent lasts for four Sundays leading up to Christmas. The season not only symbolizes the waiting for Christ's birth but also for his final return.

During the advent season, four candles around a wreath are involved in the celebration of Advent. A candle is lit on each of the four Sundays before

Christmas. Unfortunately, because of the pandemic we are not able to light candles this year because we are not in the sanctuary but online. But we must understand that the four candles symbolize: <u>HOPE</u>, <u>PEACE</u>, <u>JOY</u>, and <u>LOVE</u>.

We hope that by God's grace and mercy, we will be able to celebrate Advent season in the sanctuary next year and light the four candles for the season as our traditions demand.

Meanwhile, let us turn our attention to the Gospel reading for today recorded in Mark 1: 1-8. A careful observation does show that the first verse of the Gospel of Mark does not contain a main verb. It says "The beginning of the good news of Jesus Christ, the Son of God" (1:1)

The significance of this observation is to see that these words do not compose a sentence, they rather serve to express the title of the Gospel of Mark.

Whatever story, miracle, parable, exorcism, teaching, or narrative events of Jesus is in the Gospel of Mark, it is the beginning of the good news of Jesus Christ.

The beginning takes place in our hearing or reading of the gospel of Mark. The words of this gospel break into our lives with good news, the gospel of Jesus Christ, the Son of God.

The good news begins with the witness of two prophetic texts from Malachi and Isaiah that announce a forerunner who will go before the coming of God's Messiah.

A messenger of God will go "ahead of you" Malachi (3:1), one who will "Prepare the way of the Lord, make his paths straight" (Isaiah 40:3)

The messenger, witness, and forerunner of this time of fulfillment is John the Baptizer. During this second Sunday of Advent, we focus on the person of John. In our text, we hear an extensive description of John's identity. He lives in the wilderness near the river Jordan where Jesus is later baptized.

The baptism he offers is for his people from the Judean countryside as a baptism of repentance for the forgiveness of sins (1:4). The faith in which God's people have lived in Messianic hope serves as the inaugural word, bringing together the anticipation and fulfillment times of God's salvation.

John's baptism is preparatory in anticipation for the coming of the Messiah. John even draws people from the city of Jerusalem, the city of religious leaders, who were baptized by him (John) in the river Jordan, confessing their sins (1:5).

John's baptism of repentance and forgiveness is a call to the people of Judea and those in the city of Jerusalem to turn from their godless ways and receive the forgiveness that is present in God. Today, as we celebrate the Advent season, the same message comes to us: We must turn from our godless ways, receive forgiveness that is present in God and lead a newness of life pleasing and acceptable to God.

The description of John stretches our imagination. He is identified as a wilderness man. "John was clothed with camel's hair, with a leather belt around his waist, and he ate locusts and wild honey" (1:6).

However, the primary intention of John was not to draw attention to himself, but to the one of whom he is the forerunner: "The one who is more powerful than I is coming after me, I am not worthy to stoop down and untie the thong of his sandals" (1:7). John's role is that of a servant to the one he is called to serve.

The baptism of this "one who is to come is radically different from that of John's baptism: "I have baptized you with water, but he will baptize you with the Holy Spirit" (1:8). This is the role that John plays out in a significant way, calling attention to the one who ushers in God's kingdom. Jesus is the Messiah whose ministry is empowered by God's spirit.

The baptism of Jesus by John in the river Jordan is a baptism in which the manifestation of the Holy Spirit is evident". And just as he was coming up out of the water, Jesus saw the heavens torn apart and the Spirit descending like a dove on him (1:10). The voice from heaven confirms who Jesus is:

"And a voice came from heaven: "You are my son, beloved, with you I am well pleased" (1:11)

John fulfills the role of the one who is the forerunner, the one who is called to make known "the Messiah", the Son of God (1:11), the Lord (1:3), the one who will baptize with the Holy Spirit (1:8), and the one who is "God's son, the Beloved (1:11). Within the opening verses of the gospel, we are introduced to Jesus, and we see and hear for ourselves the one who is "the beginning of the good news" (1:1).

This is the one who has come, who is present, and who is to come again. We too are called to announce and make known God's son in this season of advent. Like the witness of John, we too are witnesses to the one who incarnates "the beginning of the good news, the gospel (1:1).

From the "beginning" the evangelist Mark leads us through the pages of the gospel with the intention and goal of seeing Jesus Christ as the one who is the crucified and risen Lord. This is not only the beginning of the good news, the gospel, but in Jesus' death and resurrection we have the fulfillment of all things in Jesus Christ.

John the Baptist leads us in this advent season to the one who is our Lord, whose birth we await and whose reign in eternity will never end. This is the beginning of the good news, the gospel of Jesus Christ, the Son of God (1:1).

But the question for us is: How do we prepare for the Lord's coming? What do we need to prepare for Christ's coming?

There are many of us who have been taken captives to Babylon (the world), and we have been deluded by the deceitful riches, fame, glamor, power and influence of a lost world. Jesus is the only way from Babylon (our captivity) to the heavenly Jerusalem. This Advent season, please come out of slavery, come out of sin, come out of the world into the Kingdom of God, ruled by the Lord Jesus Christ and experience the good news of salvation, joy, peace, hope and Love.

To do so, as you hear the Good news preached, read or shared, our prayer is that you will be convicted of your sins, repent of your sins, confess your sins, accept Jesus Christ as your personal savior, get baptized by water and by the Holy Spirit, and live a new life everyday, guided by the word of God and the presence of the Holy Spirit in your life.

Wherever you are now, bow down your head and ask God to forgive you your sins and restore you to the newness of life in the name of the Father, the Son and the Holy Spirit. Amen.

---- CHAPTER 19 ----

TEXT: LUKE 1:26-38

TOPIC: "NOTHING IS IMPOSSIBLE TO GOD"

Introduction: This Sunday is the fourth Sunday in Advent. We light the candle of hope today in anticipation of the Birth of Jesus Christ next Sunday.

Hope is the feeling of expectation and desire for a certain thing to happen. It is an optimistic state of mind that is based on an expectation of positive outcomes with respect to events and circumstances in one's life or the world at large. We all at one stage or another, have hoped for something positive to happen to us in our lives. Maybe we hoped for a good education, a good job, a good marriage, good health, a good life and a good achievement in our profession.

Unfortunately, for some of us it may have taken many years in our lives to achieve these goals or still we are struggling to realize our hope in life. Friends and family members have mocked us, given up on us, and our community or society may have counted us out. But the good news is that there is "nothing impossible to God". If we keep on hoping and trusting in God, a day will come when God will arise and shine in our lives. What we need to understand is that hope never dies. To have hope is to want an outcome that makes your life better in some way. Hope not only can help make a tough present situation more bearable, but also can eventually improve our lives because envisioning a better future motivates us to take the steps to make it happen.

Whether we think about it or not, hope is a part of everyone's life. Everyone hopes for something. It is an inherent part of being a human being. It helps us define what we want in our futures and it is a part of the self-narrative about lives we all have running inside our minds. This Christmas season, no matter what is happening in our lives that we hope should change and we are not seeing a change, let us keep hope alive, "For there is nothing impossible to God".

Our text today gives us examples of families hoping for a change in their circumstances, finally receiving God's intervention and blessings.

In Luke 1:26-38, we see the Gospel writer interweaving the stories of John's birth to Elizabeth and Zachhariah to provide an entry into the story of the birth of Jesus to Mary and Joseph.

We learn that the angel Gabriel comes to Zachariah, a priest in the temple, to announce the news that their prayers have been answered and Elizabeth will bear a son who will be one like the prophet Elijah. "He will turn many of the people of Israel to the Lord their God" (1:16).

Until the birth of John, Zechariah will be mute because of his unbelief in such an announcement (1:20). Because of her age and embarrassment about her pregnancy, Elizabeth remained in seclusion for five months (1:24-25).

Now, in the sixth month of Elizabeth's pregnancy, the angel Gabriel is sent by God "to a virgin" engaged to a man whose name was Joseph, of the house of David. The virgin's name was Mary (1:26-27). Mary receives Gabriel's words in wonderment: "Greeting, favored one! The Lord is with you" But she was much perplexed by his words and pondered what sort of greeting this might be" (1:28-29).

What Mary was about to hear was something that will change her life forever. To a young maiden engaged to Joseph came the words of <u>comfort</u> and <u>promise</u>: "Do not be afraid, Mary, for you have found favor with God. And now, you will conceive in your womb and bear a son, and you will call him Jesus" (1:30-31).

The name "Jesus" would have special meaning for her and all Israelites, because it is derived from a Hebrew word that means "savior" and signifies the promise of one who saves God's people.

Not only will Mary conceive a child in a way never heard of before, but the child will play a special role in the salvation of all God's people. Hear the message of the angels to the shepherd's "To you is born in the city of David, a Savior, who is the Messiah, the Lord" (2:11).

The proclamation of who Jesus is has to be one of the most exalted in all scripture: "He will be great, and will be called the Son of the Most High, and the Lord God will give to him the throne of his ancestor David. He will reign over the house of Jacob forever, and of his kingdom there will be no end" (1:32-33).

In Jesus, the fulfillment of the ages has come. The Messiah, so longed for in the history of God's people, brings together the reign of David and the promise of life to the family of Jacob and Israel. Thus it is no wonder that Mary responds: "How can this be, since I am a virgin? (1: 34).

The wonderful exchange between Mary and the angel Gabriel continues to express God's pure and simple gift to Mary: "The Holy Spirit will come upon you, and the power of the Most High will overshadow you, therefore the Child to be born will be holy; he will be called Son of God (1:35).

Within this simple verse, we have the basis why the Christian faith is centered in the triune God. All three persons are present in the God we confess as "the Most High", in Jesus Christ "the Son of God", and the overshadowing presence of "the Holy Spirit"

The connection back to the verses that preceded our text (Luke 1:5-25) now draws this story to a conclusion, once again linking John and Jesus in a familial relationship.

"And now your relative Elizabeth in her old age has also conceived a son; and this is the sixth month for her who was said to be barren" (1:36).

The older and once barren mother is visited by the younger mother to be in the verses that follow our text (1:39-45).

The text records one of the most touching experiences of a mother, once barren: "When Elizabeth heard Mary's greetings, the child leaped in her womb. Elizabeth was filled with the Holy Spirit and exclaimed with loud cry (1:41-42) followed by her words of praise in (1:42-45).

The interpretative key to the first two chapters of the Gospel of Luke is present in the message of the angel: "For nothing will be impossible with God" (1:37).

This is the story of Elizabeth, Mary and the faith in which the evangelist has authored this gospel. This theme continues throughout the entire gospel of the crucifixion, resurrection, and ascension of Jesus Christ - nothing is impossible with God.

The final responses of Mary in our text for today expresses the faith of the young Mother and chosen one of God.

"Here am I, the servant of the Lord; let it be with me according to your word. "Then the angel departed from her" (1:38).

This advent season, it is true that "Nothing is impossible with God". It is true today, as it was over 2,000 years ago. It is also true that somebody has to say "Yes" or else the impossible will never happen".

That ought to encourage us at this season of the year because the Christmas story is filled with miracles from beginning to end.

- The wise men see a miraculous star in the sky and travel to Bethlehem.
- The angels sing to the shepherds on the field.
- An old woman, Elizabeth, gives birth to a son.
- A virgin Mary gets pregnant.
- A wicked King Herod kills all the babies in Bethlehem except the one baby he most wanted to kill.
- The baby and his parents are warned in a dream of the King's evil plan and escape to Egypt in the nick of time.
- There are miracles galore in the Christmas story. During this season, the words Christmas and miracles go together. That is good news for all of us and very good for some of us because some of us are carrying heavy burdens today. For some of us Christmas will be lonely this year because we lost a loved-one. Some of us are out of work and don't have a single lead on a good job. Some of us are looking at a marriage that seems worse than hopeless. Some of us are estranged from members of our own family. Some of us have children who are far away from God. Some of us feel lonely and far away from God ourselves. And some of us are facing lingering illness in our bodies. And the list goes on.

But all these things have this in common:

They seem impossible to solve by any human means. After all, if human means would have solved our problems, they would have been solved long ago. Christmas is all about miracles. God specializes in things thought impossible. He does the things others cannot do. So, during this Christmas, God wants you to trust him for your miracle. But He wants something from you. What he wants from you is the same thing he wanted from Mary. Simple faith that he will keep his word in unlikely and unexpected ways. The question is: do you hope for a change in your circumstances? This Christmas, say yes Lord and pray not for more faith but rather for courage to exercise your faith like Mary, and be willing to believe in spite of your doubts. May the Lord God almighty grant you grace and mercy, to keep your faith in Him in the name of the Father, the Son and the Holy Spirit. Amen.

CHAPTER 20

TEXT: LUKE 2:22-40

TOPIC: "THE WAITING IS OVER"

Introduction: Seasonal greetings to you all in the name of Jesus Christ our Lord. I hope you all had a Merry Christmas with family and friends. Glory be to God the gracious, merciful and loving God who has given us salvation in the Lord Jesus Christ. As we close the year 2020, our text for this last Sunday is taken from Luke 2:22-40. It deals with the presentation of Jesus in the Temple. Luke Chapter 2 starts with the story of the birth of Jesus (1-7), the familiar and beloved story that includes the angels and the shepherds (8-20). It moves to this week's Gospel lesson, the presentation of Jesus in the temple and return to Nazareth (22-40).

At the point of our text, Jesus is only a few weeks old, but he has been recognized by:

- Elizabeth, Mary's kingswoman whose baby John, "leaped in her womb, and Elizabeth was filled with the Holy Spirit. She called

out with a loud voice and said "Blessed are you among women, and blessed is the fruit of your womb (1:41-42).
- Recognized by Zachariah, Elizabeth's husband who prophesied that God "has raised up a horn of salvation for us in the house of his servant, David (1:69). And by the angels and shepherds (2:8-29). The wise men will come later. Our text says "when the days of their purification according to the law of Moses were fulfilled, they brought him up to Jerusalem, to present him to the Lord" (verse 22).

Purification applies only to the mother. Luke seems to be combing two rites here:

One is the purification of the mother following the birth of a child (Leviticus 12:1-8). The mother is considered unclean for forty days following the birth of a son or eighty day following the birth of a daughter. During that time, she is prohibited from going to the temple or handling holy objects. The other is the presentation in the temple - a consecration and redemption of the first born (Exodus 13:1-2, 11-16) signifying that the child is "Holy to the Lord" (verse 23). The redemption commemorates the deliverance of the people of Israel through the final plague - the death of the first born of Egypt. Henceforth, all firstborn of Israel (animals as well as humans) are to be redeemed. The price of redemption for a human baby is five shekels of silver (Numbers 18:15-16). The purpose of the ceremony is to "be for a sign on your hand, and for symbols between your eyes; for by strength of hand Yahweh brought us out of Egypt" (Exodus 13:16).

Luke does not mention the redemption of Jesus here. Jesus needs no redemption, because he will always belong to God (verse 21).

A third requirement for a baby boy is circumcision. That took place earlier, on the eight day after Jesus' birth (verse 21).

Luke makes it clear that Jesus, from the very beginning, is obedient to the Law of Moses, He also confirms the devotion of Mary and Joseph to the law, mentioning it three times in verses 22-24, verses 27 and 29. We will soon learn that Joseph and Mary go to Jerusalem every year for Passover (2:41-42).

What our text is teaching us is that today, we often ignore such observances or handle them poorly in our lives. What we forgot is that God has planted something in our hearts that needs to find meaning amid the everyday events of life.

As the church, we need to help people to observe the passages of Life (birth, coming of age, marriage, illness, death) in ways that acknowledge the Lord - and that lend those passages dignity.

And as individuals we need to make space in our lives to express thanksgiving for the blessings we have received and to praise God for his mercies and to ask God for guidance and forgiveness. Where possible, we need to eat together as a family, and we need to take the opportunity to express thanks for the food and for the people around the table. We need to pray for our children and teach them to pray. We need to make God a part of our daily lives.

To understand our text further, let us ask ourselves what children do on Christmas morning. I believe that we see our children and grandchildren dashing from their beds to the living room or family room or wherever the presents are to see what gifts they have gotten. And what they will be thinking when they finally get out of bed is "the waiting is finally over". Well, our text says about two thousand years ago, there was an elderly man by the name Simeon, and the Lord had made it clear to him that he was going to see face to face the long awaited Messiah of the Jewish people. He was not going to die until he had seen the Messiah.

And at this point in Simeon's life, he had become an old man, so he knew that it was to be happening soon. He was not going to live much longer. And that is the encounter we see today when in Simeon's life - at last the waiting would be over.

Our text says that 40 days after Jesus' birth, Joseph and Mary come to the temple for a dedication and purification ceremony (verse 22). Now in verse

25 as they come to the temple, that is where they connect with Simeon. Simeon was a devout Jew. He is a righteous man. He is a good man. And the Holy Spirit made it clear, when he was much younger, that he was not going to die before he would come face to face with the Messiah.

So here is Simeon being led by the Holy Spirit to the temple at the very time when Joseph and Mary are coming for the dedication and purification ceremony when Jesus is 40 days old. And when he had seen the child Jesus, the Messiah, he blesses God for realizing that at last, the waiting is over.

He prays "Now Lord, You are releasing Your bond-servant to depart in peace, According to your word. For my eyes have seen your salvation".

We note that as Simeon is blessing God for the privilege of knowing that the waiting is over in his life and he had seen the Messiah, he realizes Jesus had not just come for the Jews, but He has come for all mankind. He goes on to say that Jesus "<u>is the glory of Your people Israel</u>". The Jewish people have contributed much to the world in which we live, but the greatest contribution of the Jewish people, of Israel, is the Messiah. God chose the Hebrew people to give the world a savior.

What I want us to meditate on this morning is the haunting words Simeon shared with Mary: Simeon blessed the child and said to Mary His mother:

"Behold, this Child is appointed for the fall and rise of many in Israel, and for a sign to be opposed - and a sword will pierce even your own soul to the end that thoughts from many hearts may be revealed" (verse 34).

Jesus' coming divides all the world into two groups: the fall of many - those who miss it, those that stay in the darkness, those who never have a saviour for their sins, those without Savior who wind up spending eternity in hell.

But Jesus would also be the rise of many - those who come to receive Christ, to trust in Christ as the One who can save them from sin and death and hell and give them victory over the grave, and give us the gift of eternal life. Jesus is the cause of all humankind being in two groups. The question is: Which group are you?

Simeon very prophetically, made it clear that Jesus would be the fall and rise of so many. But not only that, like Mary, one day your heart is going to be pierced like a sword piercing it. And when Mary, with a mother's love, was at the cross when Jesus had the spikes nailed into His wrists and the spikes nailed into His feet and the spear thrust into His side, she would remember those words. It would be like a sword in her heart, seeing her son suffering so, but remembering that from the time Jesus entered this world, He came to be her savior as well.

As she reflected on the words of Simeon, she knew why Jesus was dying. <u>He was dying for her</u>. He was dying for you. He was dying for me. He was dying for all mankind. And all mankind has to make a decision in how to respond to the gift of Christmas which is Jesus.

Those of us who have received Christ as our Savior and Lord, we know the waiting is over in our life when it comes to realizing that we have received salvation, that we have been forgiven of our sins though we don't deserve it.

We have been made right with God though we don't deserve it.

We have received the gift of eternal life though we don't deserve it.

For those of us who have trusted Christ and received the gift of Christmas, which is Jesus, we know the waiting is over. We don't have to wait for all this, we have received it.

But for many of you here, there are some of you, who have not received the gift of Christmas, the gift of Jesus, who have not put your faith in Christ as your only hope for salvation from sin and death and hell. Who have not put your faith in Christ as the only hope for receiving the gift and eternal life and victory over death.

Today, can be your Simeon moment, when you finally see Jesus and believe.

And if you do, you will instantly know that the waiting is over in your life.

- The waiting is over of wondering if you can ever get yourself free of this nagging guilt, of this nagging emptiness in your heart.
- The waiting is over in realizing that you would have found the ultimate meaning and purpose of life and it comes from knowing Jesus as your savior and Lord.
- This Christmas, we all received some wonderful gifts and presents from friends, love ones and from our Church family. But the best gift of all is the gift of Jesus Christ given to us by our Father in heaven:

"For God so loved the world that he gave His only son, that whosoever believes in Him should not perish but have eternal life" (John 3:16). Please do not enter into the new year without Christ in your life. He is the best. I pray that you receive this wonderful gift of God during this Advent season in the name of the Father, the Son and the Holy Spirit. Amen.

Chapter 21

TEXT: JOHN 1:1-8, 10-18

TOPIC: "WALK IN THE LIGHT"

Introduction: Greetings in the name of our Lord and Savior Jesus Christ. I wish you all a Happy New Year and pray for God's grace, mercy and love upon us as we journey together in 2021. In a world full of darkness, we need God's light to shine in our lives journey. The Bible definition of darkness both in the Old and New Testaments is an evocative word. If light symbolizes God, darkness connotes everything that is anti-God: the wicked, judgment, and death. Salvation brings light to those in darkness (Isaiah 9:2)

Although darkness is opaque to man, it is transparent to God (Psalm 139:12).

God rules the Darkness. There is no thought that darkness is equal in power to God's light. The absolute, sovereign God rules over the darkness and powers of evil. God rules over darkness because He knows the darkness. He knows where it is (Job 34:22) and what it contains (Dan 2:22). God rules over darkness because He created it (Isaiah 45:7) (Amos 4:13). God uses the darkness for His own purposes: to hide himself from the sight of man (Psalm 18:11) and to bring his judgment on evil doers (Deut 28:28-29), evil nations and false prophets (Jer 23:12).

It is to this background of darkness that our text today speaks of Jesus as the <u>Light of the World.</u>

Beyond the physical element, light in the Bible stands for spiritual illumination and truth. It encompasses all that is pure, good, and holy, as opposed to the darkness of evil. God's Word is a lamp to my feet and a light for my path (Psalm 119:105). It guides us in following his commands throughout our lives.

In John 1:1-8, 10-18, the Gospel writer John, tells us that Jesus is the Word, Light and Life of the world. He says in "the beginning was the Word, and the Word was with God, and the Word was God" (1:1). He makes us understand that the Word, Jesus, existed before the world was created. Jesus is the Son of God, Jesus is God. Jesus is Life (1:4), Light (1:4, 9) and that there is the struggle between light and darkness (1:5). He makes us understand the power of light over darkness (1:5).

The overarching theme of John's Gospel is that the Word who was in the beginning with God, and was God, became flesh and lived among us full of grace and truth (verse 14).

Jesus came to give light to those who sit in darkness and to show us the way to God. But the surprising thing is that "those who were His own did not receive him (verse 11)"

These will include those charged with the spiritual welfare of the Jewish community, the scribes, Pharisees, and priest, men who should have seen the light in Jesus' life who should have welcomed him with open arms. But they did not yet the blessing is that "as many received Him the gave the right to become God's children (verse 12).

John makes it clear to us what his purpose of writing this Gospel is: "These are written that you may believe that Jesus is the Messiah, the Son of God, and that believing you may have life in His name" (John 20:31).

As we live our lives and journey through this dark world, God loves us and has revealed Himself unto us through his Son, Jesus Christ, so that those who believe in Him will not perish but have eternal life. To convince us of the deity of His Son, God through John the writer, tells us that Jesus is eternal (John 1:1-2), Jesus is the Word, Jesus is distinct, from the Father (1:1), Jesus is God (1:18), Jesus is the Creator (1:3), Jesus is the Life, the source of all spiritual life (Ju 1:4, 14:6). Jesus is God in flesh (1:14), Jesus shares the Father's glory and reveals God's grace, and love, Jesus is Eternal, which means He possesses the quality of eternality.

1. So as we live our lives this year, and beyond, God is revealing Himself to us again through Jesus his Son who is the light of the world and invites us to walk in the light Jesus and darkness will not destroy us. The question therefore is: Are we ready and committed to give our lives to Jesus Christ, to transform us and to be a light unto our path.

    If you are not convinced that walking in the light is beneficial to you let me help you see the benefits of walking in the light.

    If we walk in the light, there is a presence of God in those who walk in the light. We may not always be aware of the light but it is evident in how we speak, act, and think about life, work, family, and the Christian faith. The light that is within all believers exposes and drives out the darkness. Satan and his demons cannot stand the light of Jesus Christ in His people.

    So the Bible says if we walk in the light, it keeps us from stumbling." For you have delivered me from death and my feet from stumbling, that I may walk before God in the light of life (Psalm 56:13).

    When we walk in the light of Jesus Christ, we do not stumble in sinful choices. We are compelled by the light to recognize and resist the temptations of the flesh. Our decisions to walk away or to walk towards sins will have an effect on the brightness of the light in our lives.

2. When we walk in the light, we will be blessed.
"Blessed are those who have learned to acclaim you, who walk in the light of your presence, Lord (Psalm 89:15)." Being in the Light of Jesus Christ reveals the favor of God in our daily walk. The blessing of the light is so much more than material things: rather it is the Lord's presence and peace that hovers over us at home, work and community. What a blessing to have the presence of God over us in all we do!

3. It is better to walk in the light instead of darkness.
Isaiah 9:2 says

"The people walking in darkness have seen a great light, on those living in the land of deep darkness a light has dawned".

Many of us can remember that moment of turning from darkness to the light. In our sinfulness the darkness was normal and we accepted it as a part of our lives. However, because our hearts were ready the light was not piercing pain in our spiritual eyes rather it was a warm and welcoming light of hope.

Light brings hope. Darkness brings fear and death. None of us will drive at night without our headlights on. Neither can we live in this world without the light of Jesus.

4. Jesus is the light of the World.
In John 8:12, we read "I am the light of the world. Whoever follows me will never walk in darkness, but will have the light of life".

In this generation, many call themselves the "light" but they are counterfeits. Many people fall away from God. The light of Jesus does not excuse our sins, but instead His sacrifice on the cross, brings us to a place of repentance with a desire to change the course. Jesus will always lead us in the right direction for God's purpose.

5. <u>The word of God commands us to walk as children of the light</u>.
   The bible says:
   "You are going to have the light just a little while longer. Walk while you have the light, before darkness overtakes you. Whoever walks in the dark does not know where they are going. Believe in the light while you have light, so that you may become children of light (John 12:35-36).

   As children of the light, we obey the precepts of our heavenly Father and resist the temptation to disobey. We are children of light when we obey what the Bible teaches and walk in faith. By following the light, we move in the right direction even though we do not always see the next steps.

6. Lastly, when we walk in the light, we have the right relationship with others.
   "But walk in the light, as he is in the light, we have fellowship with one another, and the blood of Jesus, his Son, purifies us from all sin" (1 John 1:7).

   Constant conflict, backbiting, and strife cannot survive in the light. Only those who constantly walk in the light of Christ can enjoy fruitful and loving relationships. The fellowship and love that we have for the people of God is revealed as the light shines from within. We no longer stay committed to an unforgiving nor unloving attitude because the light would not tolerate it. To walk therefore in the light is to have a daily commitment to living out a righteous life. Those who are compelled to walk in the light resist fellowship with the darkness of the devil, the world, or the flesh.

   Walking in the light renews and refreshes us within so that we are empowered to be a refreshment to those around us. John invites us to walk in the Light - Jesus.

The choice is before us: To either, <u>walk-in the light</u> <u>or stay in darkness</u>. "Walk in the light or stay in darkness. "In the beginning was the Word, and the word was with God, and the Word was God."

In him was life, and life was the light of men. (John 1:4).

May the Lord grant us wisdom and boldness to walk in the light throughout our earthly life in the name of the Father, Son and the Holy Spirit. Amen.

CHAPTER 22

TEXT: MARK 1:4-11

TOPIC: "HAVE YOU BEEN BAPTIZED?"

Introduction: Warm greetings in the name of our Lord and Saviour Jesus Christ. I hope you all had a good week by the grace, mercy and love of God. To those of you who celebrated your birthday during the week: "Happy Birthday to you. May the Lord grant you a happy, long, healthy, and prosperous life in the years ahead."

According to our lectionary readings this year, we are in the season of Epiphany. Epiphany means "appearance". It is the post-Christmas in which the church dwells on just who it is that appeared amongst us.

Throughout the Epiphany season, we will be progressively unveiling more and more about Jesus. Today, as we read of Jesus' Baptism, we hear the voice from heaven, which says, "This is my son". At the end of the Epiphany Season, we find ourselves on the Mount of Transfiguration, and again the voice declares, "This is my son".

In our text, we turn our attention to Christ's Baptism.

Maybe most Christians who first read this account of Jesus' Baptism, and have a basic understanding of who Jesus is, are left with a burning question. Why is Jesus, the sinless, spotless Lamb that he is, getting baptized? What is going on here? Does Jesus need to be forgiven? For what? But to you and I, that is a different story. We need our baptism. We are sinners. We are born in sin, we live in sin, we love to sin. We wallow in sin like pigs in mud. We need a good washing off.

So Christian baptism is a gift of God, a holy sacrament that cleanses us from the soil of our soul. We who are baptized stand clean before the Lord pure and sinless.

Baptism for us is also more than a temporary fix. It is not like an earthly cleaning that has to be done over and over, like brushing your teeth every morning because they do not stay minty-fresh for long. Or like the endless tasks of washing dishes and washing laundry.

No! Baptism is entirely different.

Baptism is a "washing of rebirth and renewal".

When Jesus spoke to Nicodemus, he said baptism is being "born again". So we who are baptized - ARE BORN AGAIN. It is an action of God which recreates us to be something entirely different than the sinners we once were. "Therefore if anyone is in Christ, he is a new creation" (2 Cor 5:17). And day after day, we return to those baptismal waters - reminding ourselves of God's promise and his love and our status as his beloved children. We are free from sin, by God's grace, given in this precious way.

But still this does not answer why Jesus got baptized. One clue is in Matthew's Gospel, where John protests - "I need to be baptized by you, Jesus!" But Jesus answers that it is fitting to do so now, "in order to fulfill all righteousness". And here is the key and the significance of this baptism.

1. Righteousness comes to us only through the work of Christ our Savior. The Bible says (1 Cor 5:21). He wins it for us. At the cross he died for our sins. This was important. But also important was

Jesus living the perfect life for us. In fact, if at the cross he dies in our place, everything that leads up to the cross is Jesus "living in our place".

He fulfills "all righteousness" by standing in the place of sinners. Here now at his baptism, he publicly identifies with us sinners, by standing in our place in the baptismal waters of Jordan. And as much as our baptism takes our sins away, Jesus' baptism does for him quite the opposite.

He is, the sinless lamb of God, in a sense, he takes on our sins and will carry it eventually, to the cross. Jesus' baptism is the first step in a way toward Calvary.

2. <u>Another indicator of this event's great significance</u> is the glaring presence of God in all his Triune fullness. Father, Son and Holy Spirit all come together in a profound way here. Jesus of course, the voice of the Father, as well as the descent of the Spirit.
Few other times in scripture do we have such a clear picture of the Triune God. Surely at creation, where the Father speaks, the pre-incarnate word (that is the son) and the spirit too is present moving the waters, and bringing life to Adam's cold clay.

Also in the final chapter of our bible, where John's Revelation reveals a picture of heavenly throne, with God the Father seated, Christ the Lamb at the center of the throne, and the Holy Spirit also symbolically present in the seven lamp stands.

What an event that brings the triune God into such a focus!

3. <u>But Christ's baptism also means creation and it also means heaven for his people.</u>
For as we are baptized, we receive the three-fold name of our three in one God, becoming a new creation. And we become heirs of heaven as recorded in Romans 8:17" And since we are His children, we are his heirs. Infact, together with Christ, we are heirs of God's glory.

So what is the meaning of Jesus' baptism to us? Creation and Jesus' baptism are God's gifts to humanity. Everything God does, God does for humanity Jesus did not need to be baptized. We needed him to be baptized. The baptismal water did not sanctify Jesus; he sanctified the baptismal water. His baptism is not the means by which we identify with Him, but the means by which he identifies with us. Our baptism allows us to participate in his baptism.

Through Jesus our humanity was present and baptized in his baptism. Our humanity was the humanity upon which the spirit descended. Our humanity was the humanity to whom the Father spoke and with whom he was well pleased. Our humanity was recreated in Jesus' baptism and are a new creation, a new being.

So the question to us today is: Because Jesus carried out and completed his work, what happens at your baptism, your baptism in Christ?

At your baptism, all your sins are washed away in those Christ - filled waters.

And God says the same thing about you that he said about Jesus:

"You are my beloved child. I am well pleased with you for Jesus' sake".

And the spirit descends upon you, making you a new creation in Christ and empowering you for a life of service in God's kingdom.

So today we celebrate the greatest baptismal birthday of them all, <u>the Baptism of Our Lord Jesus Christ.</u>

It is his baptism that gives life and vitality to your baptism. If you have been baptized already, celebrate your baptism. Rejoice in it. Give thanks to God that you are baptized. Not only on your baptismal birthday, but every day. Remember what God did in your baptism, and continue to do: He joined you to Jesus forever, he made you his own dear child, and he gave you the gift of the Holy Spirit. By his baptism in Jordan, by his death on the cross, and by his glorious resurrection from the dead, Christ Our Lord has opened the Kingdom of Heaven to all believers.

Because of what Jesus began at his baptism and then carried to completion, now heaven truly is open. It stands wide open for you. But if you are here and you have not been baptized and your children have not been baptized because you have not placed your faith in Jesus Christ the savior, God is inviting you on this day of Jesus' Baptism, to come to Him and be baptized in the name of Jesus for the remission of your sin and to receive the gift of eternal life. Will you come in the name of the Father, the Son and the Holy Spirit. Amen.

CHAPTER 23

TEXT: JOHN 1:43-51

TOPIC: "COME AND SEE"

Introduction: I bring you warm greetings in the name of Our Lord and Savior Jesus Christ. I hope that by His grace, mercy and love, you all had good week. Our bible lesson is taken from John 1:43-51 and our sermon title is "Come and See"

Last week, we stated that we are in the Epiphany Season - the post-Christmas in which we dwell on who it is that appeared among us - Jesus Christ the Lord. We said we will progressively unveil more and more about Him in the weeks to come.

Today, we look at what it means to be a follower of Christ. In our text, the scene is set for us as Jesus decides to head to Galilee, and that is when the encounter with Philip begins. Right at the start of the story, John the Gospel writer, says: "Jesus found Philip"

If you go to any bookshop and look in the spirituality section, you will find autobiographies of people who have devoted themselves to the spiritual life through the years.

And very often, they write about how they spent many years seeking out a spiritual leader to follow. They may have tried or ideas of gurus, our philosophers. They may have sat at the feet of great preachers and wise teachers trying to decide who to follow.

But that is not the same for us as Christians: that is not even an option because as John says: "Jesus found Philip".

Philip did not find Christ. Christ found him. So the truth at the heart of the Christian story is not that you and I found Christ but Christ has found us. We did not decide for God, God decided for us. And the narrative that runs throughout the Bible is of a God who constantly seeks out His people. The following Bible verses remind us of how God seeks us out.

"For the Son of Man came to seek and to save the lost" (Luke 19:10).

"But the Lord God called to the man and said to him, where are you?" (Genesis 3:9)

"For God so loved the world, that he gave His only Son, that whosoever believes in Him should not perish but have eternal life" (John 3:16).

God is always seeking out His people. And that is the case right from the beginning of scripture. If you remember in Genesis 3, Adam and Eve ate the forbidden fruit, realized they were naked and were embarrassed, so they hid. And, in verse 8, God is walking in the garden and looking for Adam and Eve in verse 9. "But the Lord God called to the man, "where are you?"

Right from the beginning of time, God has been seeking us out and finding us. So let us never think that we chose God; he has chosen us! As Paul wrote in Ephesians 1:4, "For he chose us in Him before the creation of the world!"

And this is important because the knowledge that God has sought us out, rather than vice versa, is crucial in keeping us humble before God. For the bible says in John 15:16 "Ye have not chosen me, but I have chosen you, and ordained you, that ye should go and bring forth fruit and that your fruit should remain: that whatsoever ye ask of the Father in my name, he may give it you"

So the first thing we see is that once Jesus finds Philip, he issues a single command "Follow me". What is demanded of us Christians is to put Jesus as number one in our as lives. Philip is compelled to follow Jesus and he leaves all else behind his work, his family, his possessions, his ambitions. It all has to go when we follow Jesus.

Jesus, when he calls us to follow Him, does not give us any "Get out clauses". As someone once said, "He is Lord of all, or not at all". Following Jesus is a radical commitment that demands every aspect of our being. Of course, we get it wrong from time to time and fall short of the ideal - but the intention of radical discipleship should always be before us.

The second thing we notice Philip did when he set out to follow Jesus, he did not do anything else than to find his brother Nathaniel and tell him about Jesus! The first rule of being a disciple of Jesus is very simple: Tell other people about Jesus! Can you imagine what will happen in our Church if we all as disciples of Christ, tell one other person about Christ and invite them to "Come and See"? I have no doubt that there will be numerical growth in our Church. But the problem is that we are not witnessing Christ, we are not intentional about making disciples for Christ though our mission statement entreats us "to make disciples of Jesus Christ for the transformation of the world".

And what is so lovely is that Philip did not have any great learning and yet he was really effective in being an evangelist for Jesus.

The mistake we so often make is that we think we cannot tell other people about Jesus because we do not know enough or we do not know our bible well enough - but none of that matters. We do not need to be theologians to be effective. We just need to be passionate for Jesus, and He will take care of the rest.

In our text, we learn some lessons: One, to be a follower of Jesus means to be found by Him. Two, to be a follower of Jesus means to tell others about Him and three, to be a follower of Jesus means keeping on going despite the knocks and frustrations.

Nathaniel's response to Philip is not particularly encouraging. Is it?

"Can anything good come out of Nazareth?"

Philip had come running over to Nathaniel, passionate about sharing this good news about Jesus, only to be met with a really cynical response. And it happens to us often when we try to witness Christ.

I remember my first year in 2019 as Pastor of Wesley United Methodist Church. I had come in as the new Pastor, passionate to lead the congregation to a higher level of ministry. But I was met by a few members with a cynical response that did not understand where I was trying to lead the Church to. But thank God, I persevered and at the end of the year, our Church was Voted the best church in the district with a cash award and a trophy.

Sometimes, when we tell people about Jesus, we are met with cynicism or rudeness or apathy and it can be really discouraging and it can knock our self-confidence.

But when it happened to Philip, he did not get into some theological debate about the merits of Nazareth as a geographical region or its place within the salvation history of Israel or anything like that. He just said to Nathaniel "Come and See". And when it comes to evangelion, that is all we need to keep saying "Come and See".

We do not need to get involved in heavy theological debates. "Don't take my word for it.

"Come and See" is all you need to say and God will work out the rest.

Now, the real challenge to us here as a church, is a rhetorical question for us to answer. If people do "Come and see", what will they find?

Will they receive a warm welcome in our Church? Online and on site?

Will they get a sense of God changing lives?

Will they go away with a sense of excitement that something is happening here? Is Jesus at the center of our church?

If they "come and see", will they meet God?

These are all good questions for us to ponder as a church and disciples of Jesus Christ.

Therefore, this text from John 1:43-51, is a seemingly very simple passage, a lovely story about the calling of Philip and Nathaniel - but it is full to the brim with deep teaching on the nature of discipleship.

The first point we see is that we did not choose God - God chose us from eternity.

The second is that we are called by Him primarily to tell others about the good news of Jesus. Are you daily fulfilling this obligation in your life?

The third is, we are not to be discouraged by the response we may get from others but trust that an encounter with God will be life-changing for them too.

And the fourth is that we are called into a life of peace and blessing with God.

Jesus sees us. Jesus knows everything about us. Jesus perceives our deepest needs. And if we follow Him, as he says to Nathaniel, "we will see heaven opened".

Jesus is Christ indeed, a savior to be followed - and it is a lifetime's work for us to live out these two simple instructions: "Follow Me" and "Come and See". The question is "are you following Christ and are you inviting others to "Come and See"? May the Lord grant you grace, mercy and courage to "Follow Him" and invite others to "Come and See" in the name of the Father, the Son and the Holy Spirit. Amen.

Chapter 24

TEXT: MARK 1:14-20

TOPIC: "FOLLOW ME"

Introduction: Greetings to each and everyone of you in the name of Our Lord Jesus Christ. We thank and praise God Almighty the Father, the Son and the Holy Spirit for life, his grace, mercy, love and provision for us. May glory and honor be given to Him forever and ever. Last Sunday, we witnessed the call of Philip and Nathaniel to "Follow Jesus" in John 1:43-51 and how even today, Jesus is still calling us to "Follow Him". We stressed that when Jesus called us, He does not give us an option but to follow Him and that following Jesus is a radical commitment that demands every aspect of our being.

In our text today recorded in Mark 1:14-20, we witness again the call of other disciples to follow Jesus: Simon, Andrew, James and John who left everything and followed Jesus. For our meditation today, our sermon title is "Follow Me".

The Gospel scene locates the moment when Jesus launches his public ministry - after John the Baptist had been arrested.

We notice that because John the Baptist is arrested, he is no longer active in ministry. His desire that Jesus, rather than he should be center stage, is now fulfilled. Jesus was aware of the need for continuity between himself and John.

Thus His preaching begins precisely where John left off: "The Kingdom of God has come near, repent and believe in the good news" (Mark 1:15).

We have often stressed that a Christian is a person who has a personal relationship with Jesus. The invitation to the disciples and us is an invitation into such a relationship. Jesus' commands is "Follow Me".

Be with me. Get to know me. Enjoy my friendship.

Also, share my mission. I will make you fish for people. You will teach and preach, heal and serve, as I do. What a responsibility when we are called to follow the Master, Jesus.

And what a privilege!

So in our text, Simon and Andrew were casting their net into the sea for they were fishermen. Day after day it was the same thing; the same sea, the same net, the same boat. Day after day, it was wind, water, fish, sore muscles, tired bodies. Day after day, they cast the net, pull it in. Cast the net, pull it in.

If you are not casting the net, then you sit in the boat mending the net. That is what James and John were doing. Casting and mending. Casting and mending. We all know about those days, right?

We may not fish for a living but we know about casting and mending nets.

Days that seem the same. One looks like another. Life is routine, lived on autopilot. Nothing changes. We do not expect much to change or happen. This is our life. We cast the nets. We mend the nets. We cast and mend to make a living, to feed our family, to pay the bills. We cast and mend to gain security and get to retirement. We cast and mend to hold our family together, to make our marriage work, to grow up our children. We cast and mend to gain things we want; a house, a car, books, clothes, a vacation. We cast and mend to earn a reputation, gain approval, establish status. We cast and mend our way through another day of loneliness, sadness, or illness.

Casting and mending are realities of life. They are also the circumstances in which Jesus comes to us, the context in which we hear the call to new life, and the place where we are changed and the ordinary becomes the extraordinary.

These would be disciples. Simon and Andrew, James and John, are not looking for Jesus. They are too busy with the nets. It is another day of casting and mending. They may not have noticed Jesus but he not only sees them, he speaks to them.

Jesus has a way of showing up in the ordinary places of life and interrupting the daily routines of casting and mending nets. That is what he did to the lives of Simon and Andrew, James and John. That is what he does to your life and my life. "Follow me" is Jesus' invitation to a new life.

If these four fishermen accept the invitation, their lives will forever be different. They would no longer catch just fish. They will fish for people.

When Jesus says, "I will make you fish for people", he is describing the transformation of their lives, not simply a job catching new members or followers.

He could just as easily have said to the carpenters, "Follow me, and you will build the kingdom of heaven".

To the farmers, "Follow me and you will grow God's people. To the doctors, "Follow me and you will heal the brokenness of the world. To the teachers, follow me, and you will open minds and hearts to the presence of God. To parents, "follow me", and you will nurture a new life.

Whatever your life is, however you spend your time, there is in that life, Jesus' call to "Follow Me". And there are three lessons for us to learn.

First, follow me is the call to participate with God in God's own saving work. It is the work of change and growth. That work is always about moving to a larger vision, orienting our life in a new direction, and experiencing that our little story of life is connected to and a part of a much larger story of life, God's life.

As Jesus walked by the Sea of Galilee, he saw Simon, Andrew, James and John. Jesus called them. Mark records no discussions, no questions, no goodbyes. They simply "left and followed him".

I am afraid that if Mark were writing about us when he gets to the part when Jesus says, "follow me", he would write and immediately the questions followed"

Where are we going? What will we do? How long will we be gone? What do I need to take? Where will we stay? Is there anyone in this congregation who will not ask any of those questions? Surely, we would.

I tell you this, when the Lord called me out of the Army when I was 17 years old, and said he had special work for me to do but I needed to leave the Army and seek higher education first, I did not "Follow Him immediately. I lingered in the Army for another year before I finally decided to "follow him" and obey his instruction. I had doubts about His command to Follow Him to a place I did not know. Whether I will have financial security when I follow him, whether I will go hungry and whether my life will be better than the life I enjoyed in the Army. I had those and though they were never answered by Jesus, I eventually obeyed his command by faith. Little did I know that I was going to become a pastor. When Jesus calls us to "follow him", He does not offer us a map, an itinerary, or a destination, only an invitation. This is not the type of journey you can prepare for. This is an inner journey, a journey into the deepest part of our being, the place where God resides. It is not about planning and organizing, making lists, or packing supplies. It is not that easy. If anything, this journey is about leaving things behind.

Listen to what Mark says"

- Immediately, they left their nets and followed him
- They left their father Zebedee in the boat and followed him.

Second, the invitation, "follow me" is also the invitation to leave behind, to leave behind our nets, our boats and even our fathers. That was true of me when I left the Army to follow Jesus. I left my friends, my platoon, my battalion, my brigade, my rank and my army pride behind.

That is the hard part for most of us. We are pretty good at accumulating and clinging but not so good at letting go. More often than not our spiritual growth involves some kind of letting go. We never get anywhere new as long as we are unwilling to leave where we are. We accept Jesus' invitation to follow, not by packing up, but by letting go.

Third, "Follow me" is both the invitation to and the promise of new life.

So what are the little boats that contain our life? Who are the fathers from whom we seek identity, value or approval?

What do we need to let go of and leave behind so that we might follow Jesus?

"Following Jesus is not simply about changing careers, disowning our family, or moving to a new town. It is about the freedom to be fully human and in so doing discover God's divinity within us.

We let go so that our life may be reoriented, so that we may be open to receive the life of God anew.

When we let go, everything is transformed - including our nets, boats, and fathers. That is why Jesus could tell them they would still be fishermen. But now they would fish for people. They would become transformed fishermen. Ultimately, it is about letting go of our own little life so that we can receive God's life. This letting go happens in the context of our everyday activities, work, school, families, paying bills, running errands, fixing dinner, relationships, and trying to do the right thing. It happens in the casting and mending of our nets These are the times and places Jesus shows up and calls into a new way of being and our world changes.

It happened for Simon, Andrew, James and John. It can happen for you and me if we hear his voice and follow him for He has promised us: In Matthew 19:29 "And everyone who has left houses or brothers or sisters or father or mother or wife or children or fields for my sake, will receive a hundred times as much and will inherit eternal life"

The question is: Are you following Him? Have you paid attention to his call to follow Him?

May the Lord grant us the spirit of obedience to hear his call and "Follow Him" in the name of the Father, the Son, and the Holy Spirit. Amen.

--- Chapter 25 ---

TEXT: MARK 1:29-39.

TOPIC: "ARE YOU SEARCHING FOR JESUS?"

Introduction: Warm greetings in the name of our Lord and Savior Jesus Christ. I hope you all had a blessed week. Glory be to God our Heavenly Father for His grace and mercy upon us. Sermon topic from the Gospel of Mark 1:29-39 is: "Are you searching for Jesus"

For the past three weeks, we have been preaching from the first chapter of the Gospel of Mark according to our lectionary readings for the season of Epiphany.

It is only the first chapter of the Gospel of Mark, but already Jesus is performing miracles and dealing with crowds and dealing with disciples who do not understand his ministry. Already he is withdrawing to a deserted place for prayer. Already he finds himself having to reset the focus where it belongs, the proclamation of the message (verse 38).

Just a few verses ago, Simon and Andrew left their nets to follow Jesus and James and John left their father (verse 16-20). And we see him in the synagogue teaching and healing a man with an unclean spirit and demonstrating his authority over unclean spirits. Then follows our text today that takes place at the home of Simon and Andrew. It is very interesting that everyone loves it when Jesus shows up in our difficult situations. His presence makes a difference. Things happen. Mother in laws are healed. The sick are cured. Demons are cast out. Lives are changed. This is true not only for the people of Capernaum in Jesus' time but also for us here and now. He comes to our house as surely as he went to the house of Simon and Andrew.

I have many testimonies as a pastor about some houses that have been visited by Jesus.

I have seen Jesus visit an alcoholic who says that one day he prayed and Jesus removed from Him the compulsion to drink. And he has been sober ever since. I have heard men and women tell the story of how Jesus called them into the ministry or the priesthood. Some of you have told me about experiences of Jesus healing you of your diseases, mending your broken relationships, lifting you up from poverty, giving you a dream job, blessing you with a loving family and wiping away your tears and sorrows.

And I know of diagnoses that have changed for no apparent medical reason. I mean I have seen terminally sick people suddenly touched and healed by the power and grace of Jesus. I have also seen the worst.

Several years ago, I spent the night in a hospital in Georgia with a man from Ghana waiting and watching for his wife to die of a terminal disease. That night at about one in the morning, she passed. Her death to me was a holy death. I believe it was because just the moment before she passed, it was like the room was filled with heavenly angels who had come to lead her home. Even in death Jesus is present to welcome us home.

But what I want to highlight to you from our text is: What happens though when we awaken to find ourselves in the nightmare of life? You know as well as I, there are times when life is just plain hard. Things happen that we never wanted to have happen. In those times it seems as if there is only darkness and Jesus is nowhere to be seen. Some will assume he has forsaken them. They will abandon their faith. They will give up on the church and Jesus himself.

So the question for us is: "what do we do when Jesus sneaks off and we feel alone? That is the night time question."

According to today's Gospel, that time will come. Jesus will get up in the early morning hours, while it is still very dark and go to a deserted place.

This is not, however, about Jesus escaping our getting away. It is about prayer; his and ours. It is no longer about what is happening around us but what is happening within us.

Regardless of how dark it may seem, Jesus never leaves us. He may withdraw but that does not mean he is absent.

His withdrawal is in reality an invitation for us to move to a new place, to a deserted place. He calls us out of the comfort of the house into a place where there is only prayer. There, we are alone with Him and He ministers to us in prayer. That desert place could be on our hospital bed, our broken marriage, the loss of our broken relationship or the loss of a loved one. Right now, we all have deserted places in our lives. For some of us, it is accepting the limitations that age and disease bring. Others deal with broken relationships. For others, loneliness and grief are deserted places. Do you know that the struggle to make ends meet in a bad economy is a wilderness many are trying to escape? If you don't, please ask,

Each of you could name your own wildernesses and deserts.

And the amazing thing is that most of us do not like deserted places. We tend to avoid them. They are empty places that can be scary and dangerous. There is nowhere to hide.

It is where we have to face up to who we are and who we are not. There, we are confronted by things done and left undone.

And our sorrows and losses are laid bare in the deserted place. There we begin to recognize that our successes, possessions and accomplishments do not ultimately count for much. In the wilderness we have to admit we are not in control. Time in the deserted place is a matter of life and death. Yet, it is also the place where our deepest healing can happen.

And there is a price to pay for going to the wilderness. We must trade the security of the house for the risk of the desert. The wilderness prayer of self surrender must begin to replace the house prayer that only asks for things to happen or change. Wilderness prayer does not ask so much that circumstances will be changed but that we will be changed. The wilderness makes that change possible. If you are facing a deserted place in your life today, there is good news for you.

The text promises us that Jesus goes to the deserted places of our lives to draw us there. If he did not go first and if he did not invite us to that place, my hunch is that none of us would ever go there.

Yet, the wilderness and desert places of our lives are sacred places. In the desert there is only God, there is nothing but God. In the wilderness God lets you be lonely, so that you can come to know Him as your friend.

God lets you be frightened and worried, so that you can come to know Him as your peace.

In the wilderness God lets you be weak, so that you can know His strength. In the wilderness God reveals Himself as your light in the darkness of the wilderness. Himself as your light in the darkness of the wilderness. And in the wilderness, he separates you from the influences of the world as well as the things and people that you have learned to depend on, so that you will learn to depend on Him.

So in the wilderness and the desert places in our lives, Jesus draws us deeper and deeper into the heart of God, and ironically, that happens in the very place we thought was barren, empty, and desolate. The deserted places of our lives are the places of Jesus' prayer. They are the starting point for his message of good news.

Good news comes from the empty and desolate places. Jesus will leave this deserted place to go proclaim his message in the neighboring towns. Before that, the voice of God spoke creation into existence when "the earth was a formless void and darkness covered the face of the deep" (Gen 1:2). New life arises from the deserted and the empty places. The good news of Christ comes from the wilderness.

Notice that "everyone is searching for you" they told Jesus (verse 37) yet Simon and his companions were the only ones to find him.

Maybe they were the only ones willing to go to the deserted place. I wonder where the others were searching. The safety of town? The familiarity of neighboring houses? Standing in line at the door? I wonder where we will search for Jesus when the nighttime of our life comes.

When we are seriously sick, when we lose our job and have no income, when we lose a love one, when our marriages are broken, when our friends and families desert us in our hour of need, when violence and death threaten to take our lives. Where will we search for Jesus? My supposition is that we will find him if we go to the deserted places of our lives, the places that we think are barren, empty and desolate. Right now, have your trials and tribulations? Is there trouble anywhere? Are you weak and heavy-laden? Are you cumbered with loads of care? Do thy friends despise and forsake you?

Well, invite Jesus into your life, into your home, into your deserted places in life and he will turn your deserted places into good news.

Jesus is our friend who bears all our sins and griefs, who shares in all our sorrows, whose arms will take and shield us and we will find solace there.

The Gospel of Mark says: "And immediately he left the synagogue, and entered the house of Simon and Andrew, with James and John. Now, Simon's Mother-in-Law lay sick with a fever, and immediately they told him of her. And He came and took her by the hand and lifted her up, and the fever left her and she served them (Mark 1:29-31).

Rev. Dr. Jackson Yenn-Batah

This morning, Are you searching for Jesus in your deserted life to save you, heal you, deliver you affirm and love you? If so, I pray that you invite Him into your life, your house and your circumstances for healing, restoration and affirmation in the name of the Father, the Son, and the Holy Spirit. Amen.

Chapter 26

TEXT: MARK 9:2-9

TOPIC: "LISTEN TO HIM"

Introduction: Dear Brothers and Sisters in Christ, I bring you warm greetings in the Mighty name of Jesus and pray that you all had a wonderful week and that this morning you are anticipating to experience the love, grace, peace, joy, and mercy of God as you celebrate valentine's day. Happy Valentine's Day to you. <u>Our sermon title is: "Listen to Him"</u> By way of a reminder today is Transfiguration, Sunday according to the Christian' church calendar. It is a feast that celebrates Jesus' radical change of appearance while in the presence of Peter, James and John, on a high mountain as recorded in Matthew 17:1-8, Mark 9:2-8, and Luke 9:28-36. As an Epiphany story, the Transfiguration provides one of the most distinctive and dramatic showings of Jesus' divinity.

The story of transfiguration is located almost exactly at the midpoint of the Gospel of Mark. Along with Peter's confession (Mark 8:29), the Transfiguration is the turning point of Jesus ministry. Until now, Jesus has been teaching and healing. Now he will begin his journey to Jerusalem, where he will die.

Immediately, prior to the transfiguration, Peter confessed that Jesus is the Messiah (Mark 8:27-30), and Jesus foretold his death and resurrection to which Peter expressed serious objection (Mark 8:31-33). Jesus then began to teach his disciples the sacrificial nature of discipleship (Mark 8:34-38).

The transfiguration re-affirms Jesus' identity, reveals his glory, and calls the disciples to listen to Him. It validates that, in spite of his announcement that he will suffer and die (8:31), Jesus is the Messiah - the son of God.

Our text begins with these three words: "Six days later" Those words beg the question: What happened six days prior to Jesus' transfiguration?

Well, six days prior to the transfiguration, Jesus asked his disciples a penetrating question. "Who do people say that I am? And the disciples gave various answers. "Some say you are John the Baptist" they said (Mark 8:28). Now John the Baptist was dead by this time but he was such a great and powerful religious figure that some, including the man who killed him, Herod Antipas, believed that Jesus was John, raised from the dead.

Others said Jesus was Elijah (Mark 8:28). You see the prophet Malachi said Elijah would return to usher in the Messianic age (Malachi 4:5-6). So, some people thought Jesus was Elijah preparing the way for the coming Messiah. Finally, others said: "This Jesus is just a prophet (Mark 8:28).

"But who do you say that I am? Jesus asked. And Peter answered: "You are the Messiah" (Mark 8:29).

Now the Jews of Jesus' day were waiting for the Messiah. They believed the Messiah would be an anointed leader, sent by God to deliver God's people, to punish God's enemies, to establish God's kingdom, and to inaugurate an era of prosperity and peace. In short, they believed the Messiah would throw off the yoke of Roman oppression and re-establish the Davidic Kingdom with Israel triumphant over all.

But that was an erroneous understanding of the Messiah's mission.

Jesus had to correct their Messianic expectation. Yes, he had come to save his people. Yes, he had come to defeat their enemies. Yes, he had come to establish his kingdom. But what they did not understand is that he had come to save them from their sin, not from Roman domination. He had come to defeat the enemy of their souls, not their earthly enemies. He had come to establish a spiritual kingdom, not an earthly kingdom as commonly understood. And in order to accomplish that mission, Jesus had to suffer, die and rise again!

Yes, Jesus had to die in our place to pay the penalty for our sin. He had to be buried in our place to defeat the devil in his dark domain. He had to rise in our place to raise us from the dead. He had to ascend into heaven to open heaven for us. Yes, Jesus was the Messiah and he was on a saving mission but his mission would require suffering, death, burial, and resurrection. And that was a message the disciples did not want to hear. They did not want to hear about a suffering and dying Messiah. Rather, they wanted to hear about a triumphant and conquering Christ.

Now if news of a suffering, dying Messiah was not bad enough, Jesus uttered a second message that was just as bad and just as hard to hear." Jesus called the crowd with his disciples, and said to them, "If anyone wants to become my followers, let them deny themselves and take up their cross and follow me. For those who want to save their life will lose it, and those who lose their life for my sake, and for the sake of the gospel, will save it. For what will it profit them to gain the whole world and forfeit their soul? Those who are ashamed of me and of my words in this adulterous and sinful generation, of them the Son of Man will also be ashamed when he comes in glory of his Father with holy angels" (Mark 8:34-38).

So Jesus not only told his disciples that he had to suffer and die, but they must be willing to do so as well. It was a hard message one they did not want to hear. And it remains just as hard to hear today. A great theologian once said: "When Jesus calls a man, he bids him come and die" In other words, we must be willing to deny ourselves, take up our own crosses, and follow Jesus wherever he leads us. We must be willing to say NO to ourselves. We can say "YES" to Jesus Christ. We must place His will above our very own.

And that is a hard message to hear.

That is why just six days after Jesus delivered that message to His disciples, he took three of them up a tall mountain and was transfigured before them.

And in that transfiguration, the light of his divine nature shined through the veil of his mortal flesh. And suddenly, he was accompanied by Moses and Elijah. Moses was the lawgiver and Elijah was one of the greatest of the prophets. And the two of them together represented all of the law and all of the prophets bearing testimony to Jesus and confirming him as the true Messiah. When we read the Gospel according to Luke, we are told that Moses and Elijah spoke to Jesus about his departure, or the death he was about to accomplish in Jerusalem. And so they confirmed the word Jesus spoke to his disciples about his suffering, death, burial and resurrection. And then to climax it all a cloud overshadowed them and from the cloud there came a voice "This is my son, the beloved, listen to Him" (Mk 9:7).

- Listen to him when he tells you that you must deny yourself
- Listen to him when he tells you that you must take up your own cross!
- Listen to him when he tells you to follow him no matter what!
- Listen to him and give him your unqualified obedience
- Listen to him and you will find your salvation. For remember what Jesus said: "those who want to save their life will lose it, and those who lose their life for my sake and for the sake of the gospel will save it" (Mk 8:35)

So here is a simple question for us today on this transfiguration Sunday:

"What do you do when God tells you something you do not want to hear?"
Advise is "Listen to Him"

The disciples and the multitude did not want to listen to Jesus' message about him being the suffering Messiah. And so they ended up on the mountain for Jesus' transfiguration, the affirmation of his suffering, death, burial and resurrection by Moses the lawgiver and Elijah the prophet and above all by God the Father admonishing them to "Listen to Him".

And so you as a Christian today, are you listening to Jesus? Are you listening to the laws and the prophets? Are you listening to the voice of God affirming that "This is my beloved son; Listen to Him"

Everyday, God is doing a new thing in the world but the world and many Christians are not reading the signs of the times and are not listening to the Voice of God when He speaks to us.

- When he speaks about our disobedience, we do not listen.
- When God speaks about our wicked behaviour, we do not change our evil ways.
- When he speaks about our broken relationships, we do not forgive and mend our relationships.
- When God warns us against the pervasive corruption and wickedness in this world, instead we become part of the problem.

We quarrel, murder, commit adultery, practice sorcery, worship idols, create strife and are jealous of each other. There are a whole lot of things that God speaks to us about everyday that we do that are not pleasing in His sight but we fail to listen.

On this transfiguration Sunday, God is speaking again to us. Let us pay attention to the Voice of God our Father, and obey Him.

The Bible reminds us that: "In the past God spoke to our forefathers through the Prophets at various times and various ways, BUT in these last days, he has spoken to us by His Son whom he appointed heir of all things and through whom he made the world" (Hebrews 1:1-2).

So today, if you hear His voice in your personal life's situation, do not harden your heart. Listen to Him. Jesus is the <u>Messiah</u>, the <u>Savior</u>, and the

<u>Healer</u>, who heals the brokenhearted. Are you crushed by grief, blemished by Sin, afflicted by disease and sickness, listen to Him. He will minister to you.

Are you blind physically or spiritually, listen to Him. He will restore your sight.

Are you bruised, wounded, hurt or battered physically, mentally, emotionally, psychologically, or spiritually, listen to Him. He will set you free.

This transfiguration Sunday, my plea to you is, no matter what you are going through in your life, there is hope in Jesus. Listen to Jesus, listen to God. Our God is faithful. He will come through for us. In the name of the Father, the Son, and the Holy Spirit. Amen.

Chapter 27

TEXT: MARK 1:9 – 15

TOPIC: "LIFE IN THE WILDERNESS"

I. Introduction: Warm greetings in the name of Our Lord Jesus Christ. This week has been very challenging to many of you because of the inclement weather in our state and power outages. Nevertheless, we give thanks to Almighty God our Father for keeping us safe and for the privilege to worship Him this morning. Glory be to his name.

Last Wednesday February 17, 2021 was Ash Wednesday. Unfortunately, we could not celebrate Ash Wednesday as we have done in the past because of Covid-19 restrictions. Even though today is the first Sunday of the Lent, we cannot begin the Lenten Season without reflecting on Ash Wednesday. Each year Ash Wednesday marks the beginning of Lent and it is always 46 days before Easter Sunday. Lent is a 40-day Season (not including Sundays) marked by repentance, fasting, reflection and ultimately celebration. The 40 days represents Christ's time of temptation in the Wilderness, where he fasted and Satan tempted him. Lent challenges believers to set aside a time each year for similar fasting, marking an intentional season of focus on Christ life, ministry, sacrifice and resurrection.

And so today our Bible Lesson from Mark 1:9-15 focuses our attention on the temptation of Jesus Christ. Our Sermon topic therefore for our reflection is titled: "Life in the Wilderness".

At some point we all leave home. It is something we do throughout our lives. Over and over again, we leave home. We have all done it. We leave home physically, emotionally, and spiritually. We leave those places that are familiar, comfortable, predictable. Sometimes, we can't wait to leave. We are ready to go. Other times we would rather not leave. Sometimes we chose to leave. Other times the circumstances of life push us out the door. Regardless of how or why it happens, leaving home is a part of life. And it happens in lots of different ways and times.

For children it might be the first day of school or going to summer camp. Young adults move out of their parent's home to start college or go to work. The significant changes of life are forms of leaving home: a marriage, a divorce, the birth of a child, the death of a love one, new employment or the loss of employment are about leaving home. Moving to a new town, retirement, the loss of health all involve leaving home. Lastly, the major decisions that bring us to the crossroads of life are also about leaving home.

Leaving home can be difficult, frightening, and risky. It invites us to change and opens us to new discoveries about ourselves. It challenges our understanding of where we find significance, meaning and security. Ultimately, though, leaving home is the beginning of our spiritual journey and growth. We are more vulnerable to and in need of God when we leave home. Leaving home is not, however, simply about the circumstance of life. It is the way of God's people. Adam and Eve left the garden of Eden. Noah left his dry land home. God told Abraham, "Go from your country and your kindred and your father's house to the land that I will show you (Gen 12:1). Jacob ran away from home fearing for his life. Moses and the Israelites left their home in Egypt. And in today's gospel, Jesus is leaving home. As Mark tells it, "Jesus came from Nazareth of Galilee" to the

Jordan River. He left his home and now stands with John in the Jordan, the border between home and the wilderness. There he is baptized. The heavens are torn apart, the Spirit like a dove descends, and a voice declares, "You are my Son, the Beloved; with you I am well pleased". From there "the Spirit immediately drove him out into the wilderness". Baptism may happen in the river but the baptismal of life begins in the wilderness.

This story is not, however, just about Jesus. It is our story too. The Father's words refer to Jesus in uniquely literal way but they also apply to each one of us. By God's grace, gift, and the choice of God, we are His beloved daughters and sons. If it is leaving home, getting baptized, and going to the wilderness is Jesus way then it is our way too. We leave behind our old identity, we are identified and claimed by God as his children, and we go to the wilderness.

In the wilderness we come face to face with reality of our lives, our fears, our hopes and our dreams, our sorrows and losses, as well as the unknown. These facts of life are the source of our temptations. We often externalize temptations and make them about behavior. Behavior is important but the real temptations are from within us, not around us. We are either tempted to believe that we are more than or less than the dust of God's creation or we are tempted to not trust God's willingness to get his hands dirty in the dust of who we are. The temptations are not finally about our behavior, breaking the rules, or being bad. God does not tempt us to see if we will pass or failed. The temptations we face in life are for our benefit, not God's. They are a part or our salvation. We leave home and experience temptations to discover that our most authentic identity is as a beloved child of God and our only real home is with God. For In the wilderness, the old structures, the ones we left behind, no longer contain, support, or define our life. It is however, not an unchartered territory. The way has been cleared by Jesus. It is the way home, the way to God. We go to the wilderness with the knowledge and confidence that Christ has gone before us. Above all, in the wilderness our illusions of self-sufficiency become surrendered to God, our helplessness opens us to God's grace, and our guilt is overcome by God's compassion. That is what happens to us when we leave home.

The Gospel of Mark does not dwell on the three kinds of temptations that Jesus went through as recorded by Matthew and Luke. But lays emphasis on the wilderness life of Jesus for us. We can never escape or avoid the wilderness. Like Jesus, we must go through it. We must face the temptations of Satan and be with the wild beasts. Yet we are never alone. The angels that ministered to Jesus will be there for us. All we need to do is remember who we are. "You are a beloved Son of God. You are a beloved daughter of God. You are one with whom he is well pleased". Over and over, the angels will remind us. They will encourage us and re-assure us. With each remembrance, of who we are the demons are banished, we overcome Satan's temptations and we take another step towards God. That is the way through the wilderness of life.

Right now all of us who have been baptized and are filled with the Holy Spirit, have been driven into the wilderness of this world where everyday we face temptations on our jobs, in our marriages, in our relationships, in our sickness and trials, in our loss of loved ones, in societal cultural changes, in family hunger, poverty and of course in inclement weather, power outage etc. But like Jesus, the Spirit of God is with us, the angels are with us to guide and protect us.

Yet we must also be mindful that the wild animals our enemies Satan and wicked people distinguished as <u>friends</u>, <u>pastors</u>, <u>politicians</u>, <u>co-workers</u>, <u>family members</u> and unknown people <u>are with us</u>, to tempt, distract and destroy us.

But we are not consumed by their wickedness, temptations, trials and afflictions because we are God's children. He loves us and protects us every day.

We must therefore always remember that just as Jesus was driven by the Holy Spirit into the wilderness to prepare for His mission on earth, so we too when we seek God's spirit to live in us, we must be ready to set out on a spiritual journey into the wilderness of life to transform us for service to God.

What we learn in the wilderness and our faithfulness to the mission we are given, will determine how successful we complete that mission.

Jesus came out of wilderness in the end to preach the Good News to the people of Galilee. The wilderness life is not meant for us to stay there forever.

God did not leave Jesus in the desert. Just as the spirit also led him into the wilderness, the Spirit also led him into his ministry in Galilee. That same spirit pushes us into the wilderness where we can learn to depend on God's provision and we can learn to face our trials by depending on God's strength, not our own.

The sermon of Lent is a perfect opportunity to do just that. These forty days give us time <u>to seek God</u>, <u>to develop our</u> <u>trust in Him</u> and <u>to walk in His ways</u>.

When we do, then we can be ready when the Holy Spirit calls us out of the wilderness and into our purpose as Christians and as a Church.

Our purpose is the same one Jesus carried with him from the wilderness into Galilee. Christ is today, calling us to repent of following our own ways, to turn, and to follow him. He calls us to join him in proclaiming the good news that the Kingdom of God is here. As we fast and pray for the next forty days, may we hear his voice and obey him in the name of the Father, the Son and the Holy Spirit. Amen.

Chapter 28

TEXT: JOHN 2:13-22

TOPIC: "WHAT IS TRUE WORSHIP?"

Introduction: Greetings in the name of our Lord and Savior Jesus Christ. I thank God Almighty the Father for His mercy, grace and love for us. It is by His mercy, goodness and favor that we have gathered here online to worship and honor Him. May his name be glorified forever and ever. Amen. Today as we continue with our reflection on the Lenten Season, One of the most disheartening things we see today in Churches is how Church worship has been corrupted and turned into entertainment. In this sermon, titled "What is True worship?", we will try to correct this mistake and help understand what true worship means.

Worship is an essential part of a Christian's faith. As Christians, we worship God to thank Him for His love, ask for forgiveness for our sins and try to understand his "will" for us.

When Jesus was talking with the Samaritan woman at the well, he told her what God desires in our worship of Him, saying "God is Spirit, and those who worship him must worship in Spirit and truth" (Jn 4:24) So worship is only true worship if it is done in truth and in the Spirit.

Unfortunately, just as in the days of Jesus, so today many professed Christians do not worship God in Spirit and Truth. The result is that many of the worship that go on in our lives, our churches and our communities are hollow and meaningless to God. And this needs to change.

The background to our Bible lessons is that in the days of Jesus, the inhabitants of Israel, lived in a life of self-deception. And so God was not pleased and said this about them: "For day after day, they seek me out; they seem eager to know my ways, as if they were a people that does what is right and has not forsaken the commands of its God. They ask me for just decisions and seem eager for God to come near them" (Isaiah 58:2). Yet, their worship is full of hypocrisy and false worship. While deliberately disobeying God's command, they pretend to "seek the Lord" daily. They feigned delight in knowing his will and drawing near to him in worship. In Isaiah 29:13 the Lord said: "These people draw near with their mouth and honor me with their lips, while their hearts are far from me, and their fear of me is a commandment of men learnt by heart."

So Israel's problem was that their relationship with the living God had been replaced by rituals that commemorated their religious obligations. What they forgot is that true worship must involve a vibrant faith and not religious expediency. And that is the problem with many of us today. Therefore, the cleansing of the Temple by Jesus must be understood in the context of this malaise.

The cleansing of the Temple was meant to renew the Jewish faith: to challenge our institutional views of God, and to bring both passion and purity back into the worship of God.

That passion and that purity had been lost for a long time and as we shall see from our Gospel lesson, Jesus was standing in the line of Zephaniah, all the Old Testament prophets in condemning the people of Israel for their apathy towards God.

So let us review this story and see what we have to learn from it in our context today.

The Bible says Jesus went up to Jerusalem for the passover. This was the custom for all Jewish males to go at least once in their lifetime to Jerusalem for the passover. So when Jesus arrived in the city, there would have been thousands of people there, a huge crowd crammed into the narrow city streets and an incredible bustle and noise in the temple itself. A chaotic scene - but a highly excitable and thrilling experience for everyone there.

And of course, it was a time for peak business for all the religious artifact traders, selling lambs and oxen and pigeons for sacrifices and appropriate food to eat for that season and all the other bits and pieces that would be associated with Temple worship.

And Jesus walked into the Temple, into the midst of all the <u>disarray</u> and <u>noise</u> and <u>hustle</u> and the <u>bustle</u>.

And he looked around him at the pilgrims and the prayerful, the tradesmen, and the <u>bargains</u>, and his emotions rose to fever pitch. At this moment, it would be wrong to suggest that Jesus got caught up in the heat of the moment. We read in verse 15 that Jesus made a whip of cords. He took time to reflect and time to make the whip. The actions of temple cleansing were not done in the heat of the moment. Jesus had time to reflect and think through what he was going to do.

And then the anger of Jesus becomes evident: he drove out the sheep, he drove out the cattle, he scattered the money all over the floor, he overturned the tables, he threw out the dove sellers. No one was spared the anger of Jesus in that moment. And then he shouts, "take these things away; you shall not make my Father's house a house of trade" (John 2:16).

Now, we need to understand that this action of Jesus is an act of disruption: not disrupting the events of that day in the temple but an act of disruption that cut to the core of the historic Jewish faith and all it stood for. This is a moment of crisis not for the dove sellers and the money-changers for there would always be more doves to sell, more currency to trade. This was a moment of crisis for the people of God. Jesus was saying that the old way of doing faith was no longer appropriate, that the heart of faith had become lost in ritualism, that it was passion for God that had sold out, not pigeons for sacrifice. Jesus is confronting the people of God with a deeply uncomfortable truth: this was a moment for them to re-asses. The question for them is "was it enough for them to be tied to their ritualism or did they need to find the heart of their faith once more?"

What we must understand in the text is that Jesus was not opposed to Jewish tradition and not opposed to the rituals of Judaism per se. Jesus was born a Jew and brought up steeped in the law and the ways of the synagogue. And it was because he was a committed Jew that Jesus overturned the tables in the temple.

He was acting in the line of the prophets, in the line of Micah, who hundreds years before had written: "Will God be pleased with thousands of rams, with 10,000 rivers of oil. God has told you what is good; and what does the Lord require of you but to do justice, and to love kindness and to walk humbly with your God?" (Micah 6:7)

Jesus was acting in the line of the prophets, in line with Amos who challenged Israel with these words: "Even though you offer me your burnt offerings and grain offerings, I will not accept them, says the Lord." But let justice roll down like water and righteousness like everflowing stream" (Amos 5:22-24)

Jesus was acting in the line of the prophets, in the line of Jeremiah who proclaimed: "Do not trust in the deceptive words, "This is the temple of the Lord". But act justly. Do not oppress the alien, the orphans and the widow. Do not go after other gods. Then I will be with you in this place" (Jeremiah 7:4-7).

Micah knew, Amos knew, Jeremiah knew, and Jesus knew that true faith cannot ever be expressed through empty rituals but that the rituals we undertake must be an expression of the real worship of our lives, which consist of doing justice, showing kindness, humility, non-oppression, care for the marginalized, showing faithfulness and righteousness, and the point is If worship does not engage with these attitudes and actions, it is not true worship, because God is not primarily interested in beautiful worship. He is interested in pure worship. And the two are very different indeed: though not mutually exclusive.

But by the time Jesus visited the temple on that day, the Jewish nation had lost sight of the difference. Their purity rituals had become rituals of discrimination: Jews in the Inner Court, Gentiles in the outer court, Men in this section, women in that section, sacrifices the poor could afford, sacrifices the rich could afford. In the beauty of the ritual, the heart of purity had been lost and that had made Jesus angry and as a prophet, he had to make a stand.

Jesus stood in the line of the prophets, calling for his religious institutions to forsake exclusive purity and forsake a desire for beauty and embrace instead compassion and acceptance and love for the poor and marginalized.

So if we are to take worship seriously, we must be sure that what we do on a Sunday is only reflective of the values we hold the rest of the week. Our true worship is worked out Monday to Saturday as we care for the vulnerable and the weak and the hurting, as we share the good news of God's love with our neighbors, as we model the forgiveness and patience of Christ within our church, our communities, our families. That is our worship; that is the worship God requires of us, and what we do on a Sunday is a summing up, a bringing together all of that.

In a few moments, we will be sharing the Lord's supper and we will hear the words of Christ at the Last Supper "Do this in remembrance of me". The question is: do what in remembrance of me?

Is it to participate in a religious ritual just because that is what we always do at the same time each Sunday? Surely the answer is NO.

If that is what we are engaging in, I think Jesus would walk right down the aisle of our Church, throw the bread and wine to the floor and overturn the communion table. "Do this in remembrance of me, means we must show compassion to one another. Forgive one another. Tell our friends and neighbors the Good News of Salvation. Pursue justice and mercy this coming week and challenge the politics of greed and over consumption in our materialistic world. That is our true worship. If we do that in remembrance of Jesus, then the bread and wine that symbolise our union with Christ will be filled with real meaning and God will accept our worship.

As Micah reminds us "what the Lord requires of you is <u>to do justice</u>, and <u>to love kindness</u> and <u>to walk humbly with your God</u>"

The cleansing of the temple by Jesus is for the restoration of true worship of God that had been lost through ritualism. This morning, may we beware of ritualistic worship that does not meet the demand for pure worship of God. May the Lord help us to always worship Him in Spirit and truth and to obey him.

May He cleanse the temple of our hearts this morning of all corrupt, selfish, impure, and unrighteous worship that has polluted our worship of God in spirit and Truth. And restore us to true worship of Him in the name of the Father, the Son and the Holy Spirit. Amen.

Chapter 29

TEXT: JOHN 3:14-21

TOPIC: "THE GOOD NEWS OF THE POLE"

Introduction: Warm greetings to each and everyone of you in the name of Our Lord and Savior Jesus Christ. I hope and pray that you are all doing great and trusting in the Lord for your protection and provision. We give glory to God the Father for His faithfulness towards us. Today is the Fourth Sunday in Lent and we continue with our 40 days of fasting, repentance, reflection and celebration of the work of our Lord Jesus Christ in redeeming us from our sins and making eternal life available to us.

As we meet online to worship God and to reflect on the work of Christ for us, I have a strange feeling that there may be some among us who are still not saved by the Lord. And so, for our reflection this morning and to help ensure that we are all saved in the Lord Jesus Christ, I will preach on the topic:

"The Good News of the Pole", based on our Bible lesson reading today, taken from the Gospel of John 3:14-21.

In this particular Bible lesson, Jesus' conversation with Nicodemus links three related subjects: 1. The lifting up of the Son of Man, which makes eternal life possible. 2. God's love for the world, which prompted God's gift of the Son so that those who believe in him should have eternal life. 3. The judgment or condemnation of those who do not believe in the Son. Our focus in this sermon will be on the first point: <u>The lifting up of the Son of Man.</u>

The title of my sermon as I said is the <u>Good News of the Pole</u>. I know many of you have heard about the <u>Good News of the Cross</u> and are asking what is the Good News of the Pole? Well, what I am referring to is the story mentioned in verses 14 and 15, where Jesus says, "Just as Moses lifted up the snake in the desert, so the Son of Man must be lifted up, that everyone who believes in him may have eternal life". So the story is about: "Hanging on the Pole". And in both the Old and New testament, what God lifts up on a pole means salvation for God's people.

Jesus' words take us back to the incident in the Old Testament reading for today from Numbers 21. Israel had come out of Egypt, and now they are wandering in the wilderness. As they were always doing, the Israelites started grumbling against Moses: "Why have you brought us up out of Egypt to die in the desert? There is no bread! There is no water! And we detest this miserable food!"

The Israelites are complaining, saying they would rather go back to the slavery they experienced in Egypt than to have to travel through the desert like this to get to the Promised Land. They were sick of the meal "ready to eat" that the Lord was providing for them. Everyday it was manna on the menu. Manna waffles, manna burgers, manna bread. Same old, same old, every day. So they <u>groused</u> and <u>grumbled</u> and <u>complained</u>.

But this was manna sent from heaven. The Lord was providing for them, keeping them alive through the wilderness. They had to trust God to provide for them on a daily basis.

They had to trust God to be faithful and to lead them eventually into the land he had promised. But the people of Israel did not fear, love, and trust in God above all things. And so they grumbled against Moses. But since Moses was simply God's servant, doing what the Lord had told him to do, in effect they were grumbling against God. Before we condemn the people of Israel for not trusting in God, let us ask ourselves: Do we trust in God? Do we grumble against God on our way to the Promised Land? Do we complain about how hard we have it in life? Do we complain about God's provision or lack of provision for us? If we do, then we are not better than the Israelites and our lack of trust in God is exposed.

The lack of trust in God and his goodness, the idea that God is somehow holding out on us, is the essence of what sin is. It goes back a long way, even before the time of the Israelites in the wilderness. Our first parents, Adam and Eve, in the garden though God was holding out on them. The serpent tempted them to doubt God, to doubt God's word, to doubt his goodness. We all know how that turned out. Adam and Eve fell into sin, and with sin came the curse of death. And the rest is history. Unfortunately, we have all been doing the same thing ever since: <u>complaining</u>, <u>grumbling</u>, <u>murmuring</u>, <u>groaning</u>, <u>bitching</u>, <u>quibbling</u>, and <u>grousing</u> against God in everything that does not go the way we expect in life.

And Israel - the Lord had taken them to himself to be his own people. But they too failed to trust in God. They too fell into sin. And with sin came death. The Lord sent poisonous snakes among them. The snakes bit them, and they began to die. Let us notice the instrument of death here: snakes, serpents, just like the serpent in the garden that had first tempted man to sin.

The Lord here is drawing the connection between sin and death, the sin of failing to trust in God and the consequences of death that follows as a result.

And that is all you and I would have to look forward to, if that were all there was to the story. We too are sinners, grumbling against God, people who do not trust God as we ought. And the wages of sin is death.

But there is more to the story, thank God! And the story is the Good News of the Pole. Judgment and punishment and condemnation just is well deserved. But that judgement is not all there is.

There is also God's unmerited mercy and grace and love. And out of that great love, God provided a way of escape, a way of salvation. And he hung it on a pole.

"Make a snake and put it up on a pole", the Lord told Moses.

"Everyone who is bitten can look at it and live". This bronze snake, a symbol of the very sin that literally was killing them, became the means God provided for their healing. To look at the bronze serpent, lifted up on a pole, was to see and receive the salvation the Lord in his mercy had bestowed.

And that is the comparison Jesus makes in our text: "Just as Moses lifted up the snake in the desert, so the Son of Man must be lifted up, that everyone who believes in him may have eternal life". What happened with that snake on a pole would be replayed in even a greater fashion. Jesus himself must be lifted up as the means of an even greater salvation. And this story too is the Good News of the Pole.

My brothers and sisters in Christ, the whole world, not just the children of Israel, but the whole world, including us, are sick and dying as we lay there grumbling against God, doubting his goodness, skating our fist at God. That is the world's natural state, our lost condition.

We were dead in our trespass and sins. But God, being rich in mercy and love, provided the way of salvation. Just as that bronze snake, the very sin of the sin and death that was killing the Israelites, became the very means of their healing, so in the same way Christ Jesus took the sin that was killing us and thus became the means of our healing and salvation. Jesus literally embodied sin. The Bible says: "God made him who had no sin to be sin for us, so that in him we might become the righteousness of God" (2 Cor 5:21). Jesus became sin for us. He literally took it all in. And Jesus did this by being "lifted up".

Now you all might think of Jesus being "lifted up" in terms of his being "lifted up" in glory, being exalted, being highly honored. But not in this context.

When Jesus says of himself "the son of man must be lifted up", he is talking about his being lifted up on a cross, being lifted up in shame, being lifted up to die. And in a strange paradox that is the gospel, Christ is glorified precisely by dying on a cross. Christ is lifted up and consequently God's grace and mercy and love are lifted up and glorified, by Jesus literally being lifted up in the air, on a tree of the cross and that is the Good News of the Pole. And so brothers and sisters, this morning, I appeal to you to look to that pole, look to the cross for your healing. Our only hope is Christ hanging on the cross!

God has provided for your salvation indeed the salvation of the whole world. Look to Jesus, your crucified Savior in faith and believe in faith, the book of Ephesians put it like this: "For by grace you have been saved through faith. And this is not your own doing; it is the gift of God" (Ephesians 2:8-9).

Yes, look in faith to that pole, look to the cross, where your savior is lifted up! He is lifted up, that whoever believes in him may have eternal life". This is more than a snake bite you are being cured of.

You are being given eternal life. Eternal life is more than just this, some current life stretched out for a million years. Yes, this Eternal life is new life, new life with God, life restored to how it ought to be, life with no more sorrows or misery or separation or sin or death. Eternal life is the new life found only in Christ, and it lasts forever. It is life that will characterize the age to come, when Christ returns in glory and leads his people home in the promised land of the kingdom of heaven. Just as Moses lifted up the snake in the desert, so the Son of Man must be lifted up, so that everyone who believes in him may have eternal life". This is the good news of salvation for you and I. Therefore, let us stop grousing in this life. Let us stop grumbling and complaining against God. Let us stop thinking that God does not love us and that He is somehow holding out on us. For has He not promised us in Isaiah 43:1 saying "When you pass through the waters, It will be with you, and through the rivers, they shall not overwhelm you; when you walk through fire you shall not be burned, and the flame shall not consume you. For I am the Lord your God, the Holy One of Israel, your Savior?"

I encourage all of you to look to Jesus in faith and be saved. Have faith in God and trust Him.

May the Lord help us to be an example to others as we demonstrate our faith, our trust, and our dependence on God in the name of the Father, the Son, and the Holy Spirit. Amen.

--- CHAPTER 30 ---

TEXT: JOHN 12:20-33

TOPIC: "WE WANT TO SEE JESUS"

Introduction:

Dear Brothers and Sisters in Christ, greetings in the name of our Heavenly Father whose mercy, love and grace abound for us everyday. It is my sincere prayer that God is protecting, providing, guiding and comforting you all in everything you do. May His name be glorified forever and ever. Amen

Today is the fifth and last Sunday in the Lenten Season. This is the last Sunday before Palm Sunday and the holy week.

So as we reflect upon our last journey in Lent, I congratulate each and everyone of you who during this lenten season journey with us on our 40 days of fasting, repentance, prayer, reflection and celebration of the work of Our Lord Jesus Christ in redeeming us from our sins.

In this Sermon titled: "We want to see Jesus", I want to capture the circumstances leading to our text today. To understand what is happening, we need to go back and read Chapter 11

of the Gospel of John. In that chapter, we are told the story of the raising of Lazarus (Chapter 11:1-44) which caused the council also known as the Sandhedrin and the high priest to plot Jesus' death in (11:45-54).

Chapter 12 opened with the story of Mary anointing Jesus at Lazarus home, an anointing which Jesus said was "for the day of my burial" (versus 1-8). At this point, we see the chief priest are plotting to kill Lazarus as well as Jesus, because "it was on account on him that many of the Jews were deserting and were believing in Jesus (verse 9-11).

This was followed by the Palm Sunday story (verses 12-19) which concluded with these words: The multitude therefore that was with Jesus when he called Lazarus out of the tomb and raised him from the dead, was testifying about it. For this reason also the multitude went and met him, because they heard that he had done this sign. The Pharisees therefore said among themselves, "see how you accomplish nothing. Behold the world has gone after him (verses 17-18).

It is this feeling of powerlessness in the face of a charismatic, potentially dangerous figure that compelled the Pharisees to seek Jesus' death. And ironically, Lazarus' resurrection will lead to Jesus' death.

But before we look at our text, let me lay emphasis on the fact that the Pharisees and the high priest felt powerless against Jesus who claims to have come from the Father in heaven, because already many Jews are believing in him, before long, the Pharisees fear everyone will follow after Jesus, causing the Romans to come to destroy their temple and the nation (John 11:45-48) and strip them of their authority. Their worst fears are confirmed when the crowds who had been to Lazarus tomb begin to testify. As a result the Pharisees exclaimed "Look, the world has gone after him (John 12:19). And this leads us directly into our text today <u>where some Greeks came to see Jesus.</u>

There is no doubt that there have been times in our lives that something quite significant has happened. Someone said something or did something that had a great impact on our lives. For good or evil! Or it may have been some sudden realization we had about ourselves that changed our lives forever. Well, there was a significant moment in the life of Jesus too. You may say that every moment of His life was significant because He was the Messiah and the Son of God who had come to earth. Yes, but the fact is he saw something that happened as a very significant moment in His life and ministry.

And that significant moment is to see some Greeks wanting to see him.

Nothing significant there, we might think. Some Greeks as Gentiles wanted to see Jesus. Didn't everyone? But this was different because Jesus spoke as He heard this news, "the hour has come for the son of man to be glorified (12:23). This was a highly significant moment for Him. He had ministered to the house of Israel (Jews) who were meant to take the message out to the Gentiles. However, now the Gentiles themselves were taking the initiative in wanting to see Jesus. They wasted no time to become acquainted with Him, to know Him more intimately, to converse with Him. And this was a sign that His ministry was about to come to an end as the Gentiles approached him. The gospel message He proclaimed was to go beyond the Jews to the wider world. He knew that the time was soon to come for Him to die for the sins of the world.

And so He explained the significance of His death in this way. It would be a dying to release His life in others: "Truly truly, I say to you, unless a grain of wheat falls into the earth and dies, it remains alone; but if it dies, it bears much fruit (12:24).

Just as the wheat seed dies to allow more wheat to grow, that is how Jesus explained the necessity of His death. Eternal life existed in Him alone among humans. But by dying He could release that life to others who put their trust in Him.

So the lesson we learn here is dying to oneself allows us to gain eternal life. Jesus says "Whoever loves his life loses it, and whoever hates his life in this world will keep it for eternal life" (12:25)

That is what Jesus was about to do. He was to lose His life so that others might gain His life. But there is also a warning. The warning is that if we are not willing to die to self and to follow Jesus then we would miss out on receiving eternal life.

And unfortunately, we have many people who, confronted with the claim of Jesus in their lives, choose to ignore Him. They do so because they do not want to give their lives to follow Jesus. They want to be free to do their own thing.

This morning, the question is: Are you one of them? Are you ignoring Jesus in your life? What Jesus is talking about in this text is very important.

We have the choice to follow Jesus by believing and trusting in Him and following his commandments or to keep rejecting him.

If we believe and trust in Him, we receive eternal life. If we reject Him, it means eternal death.

So what Jesus appeals to us to do is stated in John 12:26 "If anyone serves me, he must follow me; and where I am, there will my Servant be also".

Jesus sees us as his servants. He has work for us to do. It means following Him as disciples, doing what He has commanded us to do, walking in his steps. If we do this, we will be where He is, in the place He wants us to be. In this life and the next.

He has promised that if we are faithful in seeking to serve Him, God the Father will himself honor us. "If anyone serves me, the Father will honor him" God honors all those who honor His son, those who live for Him. Conversely, God will not honor those who have rejected His son throughout their lives.

Two Sundays from now, we will be celebrating the resurrection of Our Lord Jesus Christ from the dead on Resurrection Sunday. Today, we have heard Jesus' last discourse with his disciples, the multitude and by extension with us. Let us ask ourselves these serious questions: "Do we want to see Jesus in our lives? Do we want to become acquainted with Him? Do we want to know Him more intimately and to converse with Him?

These questions must challenge <u>our faith</u>, <u>our trust</u>, and <u>our hope in Jesus</u>. As we follow Him to the cross on Good Friday, how many of us will stay with him under the cross and how many of us will walk away from Him and leave Him alone to suffer on the cross?

I pray that none of us will desert him but that God will give us <u>the courage</u>, <u>the strength,</u> and <u>the faith to</u> stay closer to Him near the cross of all the days of our lives in the name of the Father, the Son and the Holy Spirit. Amen.

CHAPTER 31

TEXT: MARK 11:1-11

TOPIC: "THE TRIUMPHANT ENTRY"

Introduction: Greetings to you all in the name of our Lord and Savior Jesus Christ. It is a joy and honor to see you all at Church today after meeting online for the past one year. I am happy to see you all doing well. It is amazing that for the past year, we have had newborn babies in the Church, and our children have grown during the year of our absence from worshipping together at Church.

I have often made fun of some of you women and I online by saying I am anxious to meet you all at Church to see how many pounds you have put on lost. I am glad that I see you all healthy and in good shape. I give thanks to God Almighty for His love, mercy and grace that has kept us alive and made it possible for us to meet again as a Church family. Glory and honor be unto His name forever and ever.

Today is Palm Sunday - a celebration for honoring Jesus' victorious entry into Jerusalem. While this was a joyful, special occasion for his followers, this event took place towards the end of his days on Earth before being crucified.

Many of us are familiar with what has been called Jesus' triumphant entry into Jerusalem. It happened that day when Jesus rode the back of a nursing donkey with its colt walking beside it as the people sang, waved palm branches and laid their cloaks down on the ground before Jesus.

What we may not understand is that it was not the only Triumphant Entry into Jerusalem during that time. While Jesus was coming into Jerusalem from the east, Pilate and his expanding army was also coming from the West.

Passover was a huge event on the Israelites calendar. It was that time of the year that the city of Jerusalem's population swelled from its normal 50,000 to 60,000 inhabitants to becoming a city filled with at least 250,000 some years and other years as many as 500,000 inhabitants.

You can only imagine what that would do to a city to have an influx of some 90,000 to 440,000 extra mouths to feed and to shelter for a week or two.

Passover was that time in which all Jews were invited to come home and celebrate how the Lord God Almighty has rescued and redeemed them from the tyranny to Egyptian slavery back in the time of Moses and Aaron.

It was that time they were invited to celebrate God's sovereignty and God's saving presence. It was also that time of the year to reflect and remind themselves and any that opposed them that at a given time the Lord could raise up another leader that would put down oppression and violence and allow the nation Israel to once again rule itself.

Many of those coming to passover during Jesus' time, longed for the day that Israel would once again be an independent and sovereign nation. They longed for example for the days of the Maccabees just 200 years earlier.

This was the period during the tyrannical rule of the Seleucid Empire under its leader Antiochus Epiphanies IV. Israel has been in all, over 400 years of tyrannical rule and were eventually saved by the Maccabees in a revolution.

Their independence lasted only 80 years until the Romans came in 66 BC and began conquering the whole Middle East including the nation Israel.

All this meant that by the time of Jesus, the people had been in bondage to the Romans for just a little over 100 years.

During this time the people of Israel longed for a new leader to rise up and defeat the Romans as Moses had defeated the Egyptians and the Maccabees had defeated the Seleucids.

To counter such aspirations and put down any thoughts of a rebellion, the Roman government would display an overwhelming show of force during the passover season. As the Jewish pilgrims would make their way back towards the city, they would be greeted by an awe-inspiring show of Rome's military might. It was all an exaggerated display of superior military might and power. And it was to send both a warning and a message to the Jewish people that Rome was not Egypt or Seleucids they defeated in the past.

Rome wanted them to know that they were more vicious and more potent.

So as Rome's army came marching in from the west, it was to be seen as a potent military threat to Israel.

That is the background of what was going on at the time of our Bible lesson this morning. Jesus' ride into Jerusalem was not by accident. Jesus came with his own message, His own plan and His own purpose.

Jesus entered the city with courage, with a proclamation and with a plan of Ultimate victory.

Jesus knew what was going on at the other side of town.

He knew that Rome would be sending its message of imperialism and military might.

He knew Rome would be sending it a message of no tolerance.

Jesus knew what it would take to have a counter parade coming in from the other direction. He knew how it would be viewed by the Romans, the Jewish authorities and the Sandhedrin. He knew that they would not be welcoming either Him or His followers.

Jesus knew what His little parade would be saying. He knew the danger of it all. But as we read in our passage, all of this was all planned. He had the colt and its mother waiting. Jesus knew what he was doing and he was not afraid of Rome or the Sanhedrin. And so in the triumphant entry, he proclaimed that he is the Messiah.

Jesus was telling the world that He was the One who Israel had been looking for: the Anointed One. Jesus was fulfilling a prophecy in Zechariah 9:9 which reads: "Rejoice greatly, O daughter of Zion! Shout aloud, O daughter of Jerusalem! Behold, your King is coming to you; righteous and having salvation is he, humble and mounted on a donkey, on a colt, the foal of a donkey".

When Jesus rode that donkey into the city of Jerusalem he was inviting Israel to accept Him as the Messiah. He was inviting the nation of Israel to accept Him as the One who God had sent as the Anointed One. He was inviting Israel to welcome His plan of Salvation.

As much as Jesus declared that He is the Messiah, He also declared that He is a different type of Messiah.

He would not be the type of Messiah that would free Israel from Egypt as in Moses day but as the One who will take care of Israel's most dangerous enemy - Satan.

That is what we have to remember about Palm Sunday all the way through to Resurrection Sunday.

When the crowds shouted out the words - Hosanna and laid their clothes in the road for Jesus, they were:

- Calling out for Jesus to bring rescue; salvation (Psalm 118:19-29)
- Proclaiming Jesus as a King (2 Kings 9:13)

But the salvation that they were looking for was from the Roman Government.

But as Messiah, Jesus came to earth to defeat the greatest enemy humanity had ever faced. An enemy that had tricked humanity into giving up

- Their innocence
- Their land of Paradise
- Their intimate relationship with God
- Their everlasting life with God and their absolute authority over the Earth.

This is why Jesus rode a donkey of humility and love.

This is why He was whipped, cursed and put on the cross for all mankind's sin.

Jesus was not interested in destroying mankind.

He was not interested in destroying the Roman Government. He came to restore mankind into the image of God.

Palm Sunday is part of the week called Passion Week. It begins today and ends next Sunday with Resurrection Sunday. The question this morning is: so what does all this have to say to us 2,000 years later? Well, it says to us that

1. If we want to follow Jesus, it will take the same type of courage that Jesus displayed.
2. If we want to follow Jesus, it will take us proclaiming to the world that He is the Messiah, the Savior of the World.

3. If we want to follow Jesus, it will take us making Jesus Lord of our lives and allowing the Holy Spirit to infill us, lead us and guide us. That is the challenge we face in this life.

This morning, Jesus is inviting us to go with him. Not as one who is walking into Jerusalem to die. That walk has been done. He is inviting us to walk with Him as the Risen Lord and Savior and live the Life that he died for us to live.

- He wants us to join Him in living the greatest life here on earth.
- He wants us to share His message of Salvation
- He wants us to be an influencer of Holiness in our world today.

May He grant us the grace and courage to do so in the name of the Father, the Son and the Holy Spirit. Amen.

Chapter 32

TEXT: MARK 16:1-8

TOPIC: "HE IS RISEN"

Introduction: This morning, I am very happy to greet you all in the name of the Risen Lord Jesus Christ.

Today is Resurrection Sunday and we all can shout and affirm that Our Lord is Risen from the grave and He is alive forever. I believe that we cannot celebrate this occasion sincerely without reflecting upon the Holy Week. It is the week between Palm Sunday and Easter when we solemnly devote our time to the Passion of Jesus Christ.

This holy week is very important to us because during the week, we recall the events leading up to Jesus' death by crucifixion and His resurrection.

If we follow the Chronological story in the Gospel of Mark starting from Mark 11, we find that on the Day which was Palm Sunday, Jesus entered Jerusalem (The Triumphant Entry).

- On Day 2 which was on Monday, Jesus clears the Temple
- On Day 3 which was Tuesday, Jesus goes to the Mount of Olives to have His last discourse with His disciples and the multitude.

- On Day 4 which was on Wednesday, Jesus rested. We call it Holy Wednesday.
- On Day 5 which was on Thursday, Jesus celebrated the Passover and the Last Supper with His disciples in the Upper Room. After that He went to pray in the Garden of Gethsemane and was betrayed by Judas and arrested at night.
- On Day 6, which was Friday, He was <u>tried</u>, <u>condemned</u>, <u>crucified</u>, <u>died</u> and <u>buried</u>.
- On Day 7 which was Saturday, His body lay in the tomb where it was guarded by Roman Soldiers throughout the day which was the Sabbath.

Then on Day 8 which was Sunday early morning several women <u>Mary Magdalene</u>, <u>Joanna</u>, <u>Salome</u> and <u>Mary the Mother of</u> <u>Jesus</u> went to the tomb and discovered that the large stone covering the entrance had been rolled away and a gentleman told them: In Mark 16:6 "Do not be amazed. You seek Jesus of Nazareth, who was crucified. He has risen, he is not here; see the place where they laid him. But go tell his disciples and Peter that he is going before you to Galilee; there you will see him as he told you."

So that was the rundown of the events that happened during the Holy Week which was started with a joyful procession into Jerusalem by Jesus and the crowd but ended up sadly on Friday with the crucifixion of Jesus Christ.

You can imagine the psychological, emotional and physical pain and frustration that gripped His disciples and his followers when their hope for a savior was dashed on the Cross.

Listen, in this world that we live, we need to be constantly aware that there are wicked forces that seek to destroy us in any way they can. But also there is the protecting hand of God that seeks to protect us from our enemies if only we put our trust in God.

The forces of evil; the Roman Governor, the High Priest, the Sanhedrin and the Pharisees did not like Jesus calling Himself the Son of God, the Messiah, causing trouble in the Temple, getting more followers and becoming a threat to their power, livelihood, positions and influence. And so they sort any means to get rid of Him. But as Isaiah chapter 53 points out, Jesus Christ is the Promised Messiah and Savior of the World: In verse 1-5 we read.

"Who has believed what we have heard? And to whom has the arm of the Lord been revealed?

For he grew up before Him like a young plant and like a root out of dry ground; he had no form or comeliness that we should look at him, and no beauty that we should desire him.

He was despised and rejected by men; a man of sorrow, and acquainted with grief; and as one from whom men hide their faces. He was despised, and we esteemed him not. Surely, he has borne our griefs and carried our sorrows; yet we esteemed him stricken, smitten by God and afflicted.

But he was wounded for our transgressions, He was bruised for our iniquities; upon him was the Chastisement that made us whole, and with his stripes, we are healed"

So as we celebrate this Easter Sunday, we need to remember that God is the Center of our lives, our circumstances, and predicaments.

Everyday, we get buried by the circumstances of life and God unburies us - He resurrects us. Over and over God comes to the tombs of our lives and unburies us. That is Easter. That is the power and love of God. It is as true as it is simple. That truth speaks louder than the reality of our burials.

There are so many ways in which our life get buried:

We get buried in sorrow and grief, we get buried in death and loss, in fear and anxiety, in perfectionism, anger, guilt, regret, resentment, self-hatred, we get buried in the things we have done and the things we have left undone.

Those are the stones that block our way. Those stones mark the many ways in which we have suffered death whether physically, emotionally, or spiritually.

And with each stone like the women, we ask "who will roll away the stone?"

That is what the three women are asking as they walk to the tomb.

It is not really a question as much as it is a statement about their life and what they expect.

Their life has been buried in loss, pain, and death. And they expect it to stay that way. They expect a stone of death too heavy, too real for them to do anything about.

I wonder how often we live not only expecting to get buried in our circumstances but expecting to stay buried.

We too, quickly forget that for every situation there is an Easter.

That is what the women discovered as soon as they looked up. The stone of death, the stone that blocked their way, had already been rolled away.

That is why we show up on this day, year after year. We want to know that the stones of our tombs have been rolled back.

We want to hear the story again and be reminded that the tomb is open and empty. We want to hear one more time, "Christ is Risen"

The youngman in the tomb told the women: "He has been raised. He is not here."

Those are sacred words; words of hope, life, and resurrection. Everything has changed. We are new people.

This morning I want you to recall the stones that have blocked your way: in your marriage, on your job, your finances, your sickness, your bitterness, your unforgiveness, your selfishness, your hatred, your stubbornness and your disobedience to the Word of God. And remember that

- Christ is risen and they are removed.
- Christ is risen and you are forgiven.
- Christ is risen and you are loved. Your burdens have been removed, unburied, forgiven, and loved.

These are God's Easter message to us not just today but everyday. So I wonder what you will do with this new and unburied life that God has given us through the Resurrection of Our Lord and Savior Jesus Christ.

This Easter Sunday, will you allow God to unbury you from all your sins, sickness, frustrations, poverty, pain, fear, and sorrows?

Just as Jesus was resurrected from the death, so I pray that you will be resurrected from all your troubles and fears in the name of the Father, the Son and the Holy Spirit. Praise God. "Jesus is Risen". Amen.

Chapter 33

TEXT: JOHN 20:19-31

TITLE: "HOPE IN THE TIME OF FEAR"

Introduction: Greetings in the name of the resurrected Jesus Christ. Today is Second Sunday of Easter and my sermon title is: <u>Hope in the Time of Fear</u>

Fear is a natural, powerful and primitive human emotion. Fear alerts us to the presence of danger or the threat of harm, whether the danger is physical or psychological.

The Bible defines fear as a painful emotion or passion excited by expectation of evil or the apprehension of impending danger. In 2 Timothy 1:7, we are told that God has not given us the spirit of fear, but of power, and of love, and of a sound mind".

Nevertheless, it is apparent that all of us, even though we are Christians, entertain fear in our lives daily. It could be fear of rejection, loneliness, disappointment, pain, sickness, death, failure in life, or losing our freedom. This list may not be exhaustive because we all have our fears and your list would not be the same as mine. But we all can identify with some things we fear in our lives.

In our Bible lesson recorded in John 20:19-31,

The Gospel of John says: "When it was evening on that day, the first day of the week, and the doors of the house where the disciples had met were locked for fear of the Jews, Jesus came and stood among them and said "Peace be with you". After he said this, he showed them his hands and his side. Then the disciples rejoiced when they saw the Lord (John 20:19-20).

A week ago we celebrated the resurrection of Our Lord and Savior Jesus Christ. But there comes a time when we must live the resurrection. And that is not always easy. How can we celebrate the resurrection when we still have our fears, issues, problems, pains and sickness with us.

Some days it feels or seems easier and safer to lock the door of our house, our hearts, our circumstances and avoid people in our lives. And sometimes we just want to run away, hide, and not deal with the reality of our lives. Yet, every time we shut the doors of our life, our mind, or our heart, we imprison ourselves.

That is what the disciples did on Easter. It is Easter evening, the first day of the week, the day of the resurrection, the day they saw the empty tomb, the day Mary Magdalene announced: "I have seen the Lord".

The disciples are gathered in the house, the doors are locked with fear. A week later, they are in the same place.

It is the same house, the same walls, the same closed doors, the same locks. Nothing much has changed.

Notice that Jesus' tomb is open and empty but the disciples house is closed and the doors locked tight. The house has become their tomb.

Jesus is on the loose and the disciples are bound in fear.

The disciples have separated themselves and their lives from the reality of Jesus' resurrection. Their doors of faith have been closed. They have shut their eyes to the reality that life is now different. They have locked out Mary Magdalene's word of faith, hope and love.

They left the empty tomb of Jesus and entered their tombs of fear, doubt and blindness.

The locked doors have become the great stone sealing their tomb. They have locked themselves in.

The doors of our tombs are always locked from inside. It has been only one week after the resurrection of Jesus but they have locked themselves in their own tomb of fear.

This morning, I am wondering whether one week after Easter, our life is different?

The question is: where are we living? Are we living in the freedom and joy of the resurrection, or are we living behind locked doors?

When the Apostle John describes the house, the doors, the locks, he is speaking more than a physical house with walls, doors on hinges, and deadbolts.

He is describing the interior condition of the disciples and us.

The locked places of our lives are always more about what is going on inside of us than around us.

So the question to you this morning is: what are the closed places of your life? What keeps you in the tomb? Maybe like the disciples, it is fear. Maybe it is questions, disbelief, or the condition we place on our faith.

Perhaps it is sorrow and loss of a dear one. Maybe the wounds are so deep it does not seem worth the risk to step outside. For others, it may be anger and resentment. And for some of us, we seem unable or unwilling to open up to new ideas, possibilities, and changes.

But the Good news is that Jesus is always entering the locked places of our lives.

He comes unexpected, uninvited, and sometimes even unwanted. He steps into our closed lives, closed hearts, closed minds and standing among us, he offers peace and breathes new life into us.

<u>Conclusion:</u> Perhaps like the disciples, you have closed the doors of your heart to events that have traumatized you in the past, may be the death of loved one, maybe a marriage breakdown, a financial loss, a trusted friend betrayed you and you are not prepared to take a second chance to be hurt again and so you have locked the door of your heart.

The message for you this morning is that regardless of any bad circumstances in your life, the resurrected Jesus is ready to show up in your life and bring you new life.

Life and peace are resurrection reality. They do not necessarily change the circumstances of our life and the world. Surely there will be storms in our lives. Love ones will die. Satan will Buffett us and trials will come.

But the life and peace of Jesus' resurrection will enable us to meet and live through those circumstances in the name of the Father, the Son and the Holy Spirit. Amen.

About the Author

Rev. Dr. Jackson Yenn-Batah is a graduate of the Interdenominational Theological Center in Atlanta, Georgia from where he received the Master of Divinity degree in Biblical Studies/Languages in 1998 and the Doctor of Ministry degree in 2001 with highest honor.

Dr. Yenn-Batah is also a graduate of the University of Texas at Tyler where he earned the Bachelor of Business Administration in Finance and the Bachelor of Science degree in Political Science in 1983 and the Master of Science degree in Public Planning and Administration in 1984.

Ordained a Deacon in 1972 and an Elder of the Christian Methodist Episcopal Church in 1976, Dr. Yenn-Batah has served the Church in various capacities as Pastor, Chaplain, Presiding Elder, Mission Supervisor in Ghana between 1972-79 and 1986-1995.

He also served the Christian Council of Ghana as Acquisitions Editor and Marketing Manager of Asempa Publishers from 1987-1995.

Dr. Yenn-Batah as done extensive mission work in Nigeria, Kenya, Tanzania, Germany and the United States of America.

He is currently the Senior Pastor of Wesley United Methodist Church in Arlington, Texas, USA.

His publishes books include: "Intercessory Prayer: A New Model for Transformative Ministry" and " A Brief History of the Christian Methodist Episcopal Church in West Africa 1958-1998."

www.ingramcontent.com/pod-product-compliance
Lightning Source LLC
LaVergne TN
LVHW021708060526
838200LV00050B/2556